C000097567

The Crochet Dude's
Designs for Guys

The Crochet Dude's
Designs for Guys
30 PROJECTS MEN WILL LOVE

Drew Emborsky

LARK BOOKS

A Division of Sterling Publishing Co., Inc.
New York / London

Senior Editor
Terry Taylor

Editor
Larry Shea

Art Director
Stacey Budge

Illustrators
Karen Manthey
Orrin Lundgren

Photographer
Stewart O'Shields

Cover Designer
Cindy LaBreacht

Library of Congress Cataloging-in-Publication Data

Emborsky, Drew.
   The crochet dude's designs for guys : 30 projects men will love / Drew Emborsky. -- 1st ed.
      p. cm.
   Includes index.
   ISBN-13: 978-1-60059-230-0 (pb-with flaps : alk. paper)
   ISBN-10: 1-60059-230-9 (pb-with flaps : alk. paper)
   1. Knitting--Patterns. 2. Men's clothing. I. Title.
   TT825.E46 2008
   746.43'2041--dc22

                                        2008004711

10 9 8 7 6 5 4 3 2 1

First Edition

Published by Lark Books, A Division of
Sterling Publishing Co., Inc.
387 Park Avenue South, New York, NY 10016

Text © 2008, Drew Emborsky
Photography and illustrations © 2008, Lark Books unless otherwise specified

The Crochet Dude is a trademark of Dale L. Emborsky. All rights reserved. Used with permission.

Distributed in Canada by Sterling Publishing,
c/o Canadian Manda Group, 165 Dufferin Street
Toronto, Ontario, Canada M6K 3H6

Distributed in the United Kingdom by GMC Distribution Services,
Castle Place, 166 High Street, Lewes, East Sussex, England BN7 1XU

Distributed in Australia by Capricorn Link (Australia) Pty Ltd.,
P.O. Box 704, Windsor, NSW 2756 Australia

The written instructions, photographs, designs, patterns, and projects in this volume are intended for the personal use of the reader and may be reproduced for that purpose only. Any other use, especially commercial use, is forbidden under law without written permission of the copyright holder.

Every effort has been made to ensure that all the information in this book is accurate. However, due to differing conditions, tools, and individual skills, the publisher cannot be responsible for any injuries, losses, and other damages that may result from the use of the information in this book.

If you have questions or comments about this book, please contact:
Lark Books
67 Broadway
Asheville, NC 28801
828-253-0467

Manufactured in China

All rights reserved

ISBN 13: 978-1-60059-230-0

For information about custom editions, special sales, premium and corporate purchases, please contact Sterling Special Sales Department at 800-805-5489 or specialsales@sterlingpub.com.

Contents

Introduction

When I was a little guy around five years old, my mom sat me down with hook and yarn and patiently taught me to make my first crochet stitch. As the youngest of eight children, I was, shall we say, "energetic." That day, as we sat in a motel room in Lake Tahoe snowed in by a blizzard, she decided I needed to focus on something—anything—but when she put that hook in my hand, it changed the course of my life.

As I grew up and my crochet skills developed, I also discovered a love of drawing and eventually oil painting. I put on my most tragically cool artist's clothes and went off to art college, where I learned that being a painter could, and most likely would, lead to a life of hunger and, well, even more tragic clothes. Clearly, something had to give.

Fast-forward 15 years, and here I am using my art training and my passion for crochet to design garments and décor items for a living. Mom unfortunately passed away shortly before it dawned on me that art and crochet were a great match. Hmm, now that I think about it, it did just come to mind out of the blue not too long after that. So now I choose to believe she was somehow urging me along that day from a better place. Hooray!

Why Designs for Guys?

If you search for great crochet patterns for guys, you will most likely come up empty-handed. There are a few masculine patterns mixed in with the feminine in other books, but the time has arrived for a book dedicated to great patterns for the men out there.

I have created designs that are timeless and classic, ones where you know intuitively that if you make it for a gift, the dude is going to love it. Change the colors if you want, put in some stripes if you must, or just make it as it is—the man is guaranteed to love it. Look on the cover; it says so right in the subtitle!

If you are a guy who crochets, and you know who you are, this is the book you've been looking for. I have created designs that will make you look good and projects you will enjoy creating. If you're a woman who crochets, you'll find a collection of pieces here that will enable you to—and I know how hard this is—give the guys you love a little more class and style. My intention is to give you everything you need (except the actual yarn) to fulfill your crochet desires for years to come!

The Tao of The Crochet Dude

I don't really know what "tao" means, but I was about to wax philosophical and it sounded right. It is my feeling that crochet (like any other form of expression) should be pursued authentically. That is, be true to what you love, what stirs you inside—literally, what turns you on. As I developed the designs in this book, I thought about each one and about the collection as a whole. I made sure that I loved every design, every fiber chosen, and every final project.

I'm saying this because I want you to love every aspect of crochet too. Choose hooks that you love, that you can't wait to spend time with, that feel good in your hand. It is my belief that the success of the project starts there. I designed

every project in this book with my incredible G3 Studios hooks; you'll see one pictured on page 10. I love them so much, I sit and stare at them sometimes. Sometimes I even talk to them, but hey, I did go to art school, so it's expected for me to be a bit eccentric. Also, always use fibers you love. They don't have to

cost a fortune, but you are going to be spending a lot of time with them and if you love the fiber, you will love how the project turns out. That I can guarantee.

Of course, since you've bought this book, I know that you must love the designs. And for that, I am truly grateful. Peace.

The Crochet Dude

The Essentials

Hold on there, cowboys and cowgirls! Before you go grabbing yarn and hook, please read the following info on materials, patterns, and sizes. Then—and this is really important—read the pattern you want to make thoroughly and carefully. Look for unfamiliar steps and stitches, and then find help if you need it. Your first stop should be the Crochet Stitches & Techniques section in the back of this book. It's loaded with step-by-step stitch instructions, cool techniques, and the lowdown on how to finish your fabulous creations. If you need some more help, stitch dictionaries and online forums are great resources that can get you out of a jam. Your last step before beginning is to make sure you have all the materials you'll need. That way you can hunker down and enjoy the project uninterrupted.

You should carefully consider the yarn you're going to work with because, in the end, I want you to really love (not just like) what you've created. The color and feel of the yarn is a big part of that. To get you started, I've listed the yardage and type of yarn needed at the beginning of each project. Check out the chart on page 121 for more information on yarn types. Hit the marketplace and round up some yarn; it's teeming with wonderful new fibers from bamboo to milk, so have fun!

Fiberlicious

Each pattern has a fiber weight listed next to the amount needed. Basically, the weight is how thick the yarn is. For the sweaters I designed to be worn even if it's warm out (the Pure Comfort sweater on page 64 or The Sport of Crochet sweater on page 95), I chose a thin, natural fiber like cotton to help you feel cool and

comfortable. For sweaters designed for warmth, I chose bulkier weight yarns like wools and blends.

You can learn more about fiber weights from the chart on page 121. You can also check out the specific yarn I used at the end of each pattern, so if you are diggin' the one you see in the book, you can duplicate it by using the exact same yarn. I've used a variety of fibers, from wool to cotton to acrylic to soy, and each has a different feel.

Take the time to go to a yarn shop and dive in. Making a sweater or other crocheted piece is a tactile experience; the right yarn choice can make or break a finished project. Always—and I can't emphasize this enough—always and only use a fiber that you love. Dudes and dudettes, you totally deserve it!

Hook Size Matters!

When choosing a hook to use for your project, be sure to not only select the size that helps you meet the gauge indicated, but also check that the length of the shaft feels comfortable in your hand. This is important so you don't get easily fatigued and to guarantee that the project has a happy ending. If you're not familiar with hook sizes, check out the chart on page 121.

Instructions, Pattern Notes, and Graphs

I've written every pattern with detailed step-by-step instructions, so feel free to challenge your crochet skills. Each pattern begins with the number of chain stitches you need for the foundation row, and then continues with a row-by-row description of the stitches or pattern combinations needed to complete the project. If the project has more than one piece, I've provided separate step-by-step directions for each piece, along with assembly instructions.

The patterns in this book range from rank beginner to downright experienced, but I've taken special care to write them clearly. If you take your time and follow the instructions step by step, you can make any of the projects you want. If you're just starting out or getting back into the craft, you should definitely take a look at the basic guide to stitches on pages 122 to 125 to get you going.

If a pattern requires special stitch variations or unusual working methods, I've explained them in a separate section. Look for these pattern notes at the beginning of the project instructions. If a pattern uses specific color changes for checks or stripes, I've shown these changes graphically in an illustration or a charted graph. Sometimes it's easier to follow the chart, so if you have a question about the written instructions, go ahead and cross check it with the chart to see if it clears things up for you. Each square on a charted graph equals a given number of stitches—and that number is noted each time.

Whenever a garment has multiple pieces, a diagram shows the dimensions of each piece. And if a stitch combination is a bit complex, a symbol chart shows the exact construction of the fabric. By the way, you'll find a key to the symbols used in these charts in the back of the book on page 121.

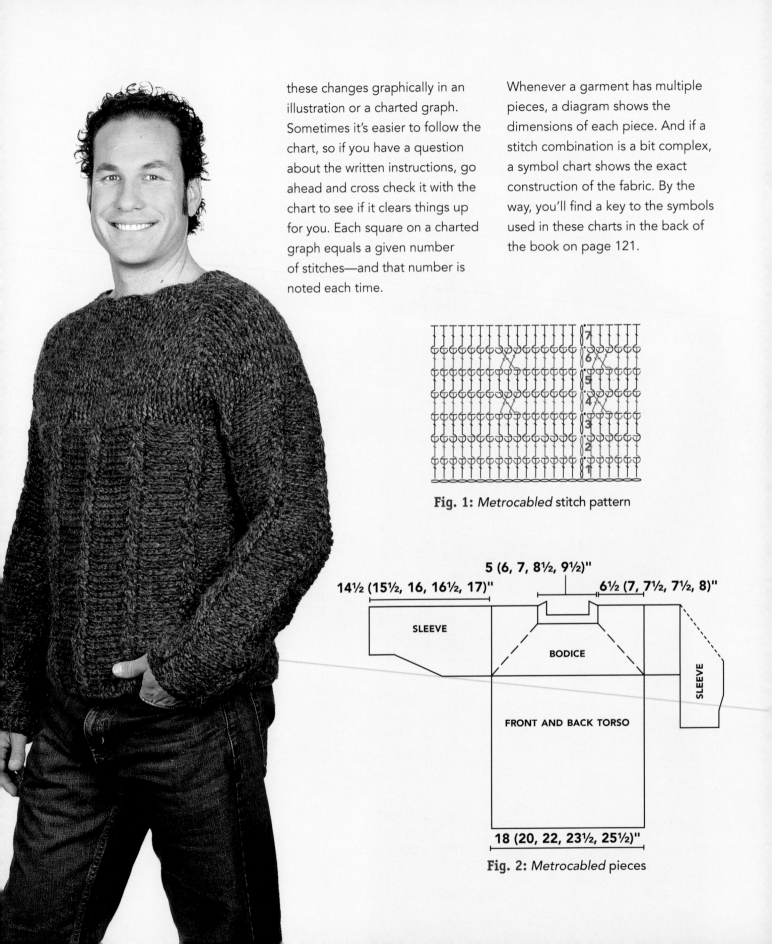

Fig. 1: *Metrocabled* stitch pattern

5 (6, 7, 8½, 9½)"

14½ (15½, 16, 16½, 17)"

6½ (7, 7½, 7½, 8)"

SLEEVE

BODICE

SLEEVE

FRONT AND BACK TORSO

18 (20, 22, 23½, 25½)"

Fig. 2: *Metrocabled* pieces

Choosing the Right Size

Perhaps you aren't accustomed to having this many projects for guys all in one place (even though you and I both know that you have been wanting men's crochet designs for years now). Let me point out a few things to keep in mind.

It seems obvious, but choosing the correct size will help you to create a garment you (or your loved one) will love to wear over and over again. I took special care to ensure that these clothes are comfortable and good-looking, especially for the larger sizes. I included the added length right in the pattern, so the garments will be comfortable even for big guys.

Abbv. Spkn Here

As you probably know—or will find out very soon in this book—the language of crochet instructions uses a lot of abbreviations. Or to put it another way, when I write "yo" in a project I'm really saying "yarn over," and not doing my awesome Stallone-as-Rocky impression. Abbreviations are great for keeping instructions short, but if any unfamiliar ones are making you scratch your head, just look them up in the chart on page 120.

If you are making one of the sweaters for yourself, a great way to choose the size that is right for you is to use your favorite shirt or sweater . . . you know, the one that the womenfolk in your life have been trying for years to secretly throw away, but you always find it in time, pull it out of the trash, wash it, and wear it anyway, much to their dismay? Why not just get its size? Measure across, right under the sleeves, and use that chest measurement as your rough guide to choose the right size sweater to make. It's that simple.

Remember when I said earlier that I designed the bigger sizes with extra length for maximum comfort? Now it's time to admit that I wrote all the sweater patterns so that the sleeves will be long. I like long sleeves. There really isn't anything more uncomfortable than sleeves that ride up when I'm working on a project or playing a sport. It's easier to roll up your sleeves when you need to. And, once you've finished making a sweater, making the sleeves longer really isn't a good option.

If you are making a sweater as a gift, here is a basic chart to use:

Men's Sweater Sizes

Size	Chest	Back to Hip Length
S	38	25 " (63.5 cm)
M	40	26½" (67.3 cm)
L	42	27 " (68.6 cm)
XL	44	27½" (69.9 cm)
XXL	46	28½" (72.4 cm)

I designed some sweaters to be loose (like Pure Comfort on page 64) and some to be form-fitting (like The Sport of Crochet on page 95). Compare the chest size from the chart to the finished measurements in the pattern. If the pattern is about 2 to 4 inches (5 to 10 cm) bigger than the chest size in the chart, the resulting sweater should fit comfortably. So if you're making a sweater as a gift and you don't know the exact size, here's my advice: when in doubt, always go for the bigger size!

Projects

Sweaters? Hats? Accessories? Turn the page to find them all! This book features 27 projects, each marked as easy (Beginner), a little more advanced (Intermediate), or very advanced (Expert). If you're new to the craft, start with the easier ones toward this end of the book. As you gain experience and expertise, continue to challenge yourself with the more difficult projects. Go grab yarn and hook and get busy!

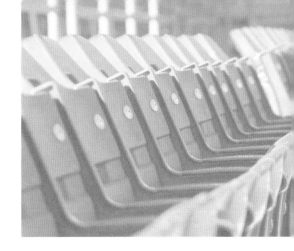

Head Banned

Sitting in the stands one freezing November day, I was sure this would be the homecoming my ears fell off, and I would have to carry them home to stick them back on later. No more! I've made this band in my old school colors, but you can change yarns if you root for someone other than the ol' Red and White.

Instructions

First Half

With A, ch 17.

Row 1 (RS): Sc in 2nd ch from hook and in each ch across, turn—16 sc.

Rows 2–12: Ch 1, sc in BL of each sc across, turn.

Rows 13–17: Ch 1, working in BL of sts, sc in first sc, sc2tog in next 2 sts, sc in each sc across to within last 3 sts, sc2tog in next 2 sts, sc in last sc, turn—6 sc rem at end of row 17.

Rows 18–29: Ch 1, sc in BL of each st across, turn.

Fasten off.

Skill Level
Beginner

Finished Size
21"/53.5cm circumference—one size fits most ears

You Will Need
Color A: 38yd/35m of 🔢 super bulky weight yarn
Color B: 8yd/7.5m of 🔢 super bulky weight yarn
Hook: 6.50mm (size K-10 ½ U.S.) (*or size to obtain gauge*)
Yarn needle
Team spirit and snow (optional)

Stitches Used
Chain stitch (ch)
Half double crochet (hdc)
Single crochet (sc)
Slip stitch (sl st)

Special Stitch
Single crochet two together (sc2tog): (Insert hook in next st, yo, draw yarn through st) twice, yo, draw yarn through 3 lps on hook.

Gauge
13 sts x 11 rows = 4"/10cm in sc in BL only
Always take time to check your gauge.

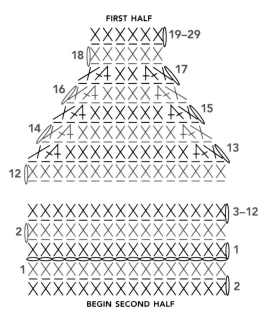

Fig. 1: Stitch pattern for first half

Second Half

Row 1: With RS facing, working across opposite side of foundation ch, join A with sc in the 1st foundation ch, sc in each ch across, turn—16 sc.

Rows 2–29: Rep rows 2–29 of First Half. Fasten off.

Assemble

Fold project in half along foundation ch with RS together, whipstitch rows 29 together to form headband. Turn headband RS out.

Finishing

FIRST EDGING

Rnd 1: With RS facing, join A with sc along one side edge, sc evenly around one side of headband, slip st to first sc to join. Fasten off.

Rnd 2: With WS facing, join B with sl st to FL of any st in rnd 1 of edging, ch 2, hdc in FL of each sc around, sl st in top of beg ch-2 to join. Fasten off.

SECOND EDGING

Rep First Edging on other side edge of headband.

Weave in ends.

Yarn Used

COLORWAY I:

Caron Simply Soft Quick, 100% acrylic, 3oz/85g = 50yd/46m per skein

(A) 1 skein, Navy (#0005)

(B) 1 skein, Mango (#0017)

COLORWAY II:

Caron Simply Soft Quick, 100% acrylic, 3oz/85g = 50yd/46m per skein

(A) 1 skein, Autumn Red (#0007)

(B) 1 skein, White (#0001)

Autowipen

Nothing will clean your awesome auto like a big rag made from 100-percent cotton. These three rags in ascending sizes have stitch combos that create the perfect texture to give your ride a shiny gloss your friends will envy.

Skill Level
Beginner

Finished Size
Three designs in three different sizes:
Small Rag: 14"/35.5cm square
Medium Rag: 15"/38cm square
Large Rag: 16"/40.5cm square

You Will Need
• For small rag: 188yd/172m of 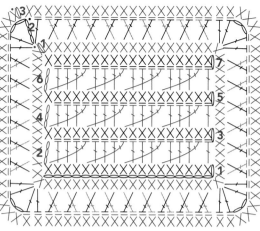 lightweight yarn, cotton
• For medium rag: 188yd/172m of lightweight yarn, cotton
• For large rag: 314yd/288m of lightweight yarn, cotton
Hook: 5.00mm (size H-8 U.S.) (*or size to obtain gauge*)
Yarn needle
Cool car (optional)

Stitches Used
Chain stitch (ch)
Double crochet (dc)
Single crochet (sc)
Slip stitch (sl st)

Special Stitches
Crossed double crochet (X-st): Sk 1 st, dc in next st, dc in last skipped st.
Piggyback double crochet (pbdc): Dc in st indicated, dc around the post of dc just made.
Front post treble crochet (FPtr): Yo (twice), insert hook from front to back to front again around the post of next designated st, yo, draw yarn though st, (yo, draw yarn through 2 loops on hook) 3 times, sk st behind FPtr just made.
Reverse single crochet (reverse sc): Working from left to right, insert hook from front to back through next st to the right, yo, draw yarn though st, yo, draw yarn through 2 lps on hook.

Gauge
16 sts x 7 rows = 4"/10cm in dc
Always take time to check your gauge.

Instructions

Small Rag

Ch 58.

Row 1: Sc in 2nd ch from hook and in each ch across, turn—57 sc.

Row 2: Ch 3, sk first sc, *dc in next 3 sts, working behind sts just made, dc in last skipped st, sk next sc; rep from * across, dc in last st, turn.

Row 3: Ch 1, sc in BL of each st across, turn.

Rows 4–31: Repeat rows 2–3.

Do not fasten off.

BORDER

Rnd 1: Ch 1, 2 sc in same st, work 42 sc evenly along side edge of rag, 3 sc in corner st, sc in each foundation ch along bottom edge of rag, 3 sc in corner, 42 sc evenly along side edge of rag, 3 sc in corner st, sc in each st across top of rag, work 1 more sc in same st as beg 2 sc, sl st in first sc to join.

Rnd 2: Ch 5, 2 dc in same sc, X-st across to next corner sc, *(2 dc, ch 2, 2 dc) in corner sc, X-st across to next corner sc; rep from * 3 times, work 1 more dc in same st as beginning, sl st in 3rd ch of beg ch-5 to join.

Rnd 3: Sl st in corner space, ch 1,

BORDER

Fig. 1: Small Rag stitch pattern

*3 sc in corner ch-2 space, sc in BL of each st across to next corner; rep from * around, sl st in first sc to join.

Fasten off.

Weave in ends.

Medium Rag

Ch 58.

Row 1: Sc in 2nd ch from hook and in each ch across, turn—57 sts.

Row 2: Ch 4, sk 1st 2 sts, *pbdc in next sc, sk next sc; rep from * across to last sc, dc in last sc, turn—27 pbdc.

Row 3: Ch 4, sk first 2 sts, *pbdc in next st, sk next st; rep from * across, dc in 3rd ch of beg ch-4, turn.

Rows 4–24: Rep row 3.

Row 25: Ch 1, sc in each st across to ch, sc in next ch-1 space, sc in 3rd ch of beg ch-4.

Do not fasten off.

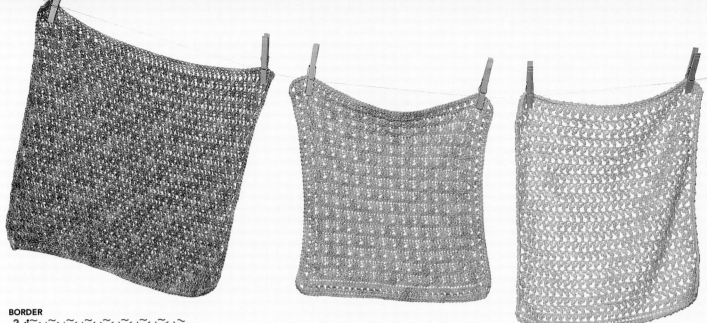

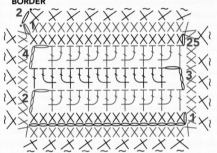

Fig. 2: Medium Rag stitch pattern

BORDER

Rnd 1: Ch 1, sc evenly around entire project working 3 sc in each corner st, sl st to 1st sc, do not turn.

Rnd 2: Ch 1, working from left to right, sk 1st sc, *reverse sc in next sc, sk next sc; rep from * around, sl st in first reverse sc to join.

Fasten off.

Weave in ends.

Large Rag

Ch 62.

Row 1: Dc in 4th ch from hook and in each ch across, turn—60 dc.

Row 2: Ch 1, sc in each st across, turn.

Row 3: Ch 2, *FPtr around the post of next corresponding dc 2 rows below, sk st behind FPtr just made**, dc in next st on current row; rep from * across, ending last rep at **, hdc in last sc, turn.

Row 4: Ch 1, sc in each st across, turn.

Row 5: Ch 2, *dc in next st**, FPtr around the post of next corresponding dc 2 rows below, sk st behind FPtr just made; rep from * across, ending last rep at **, hdc in last sc, turn.

Row 6: Ch 1, sc in each st across, turn.

Rows 7–42: Repeat rows 3–6.

Do not fasten off.

BORDER

Rnd 1: Ch 1, sc evenly around entire project working 3 sc in each corner st, sl st in first sc to join. Fasten off.

Weave in ends.

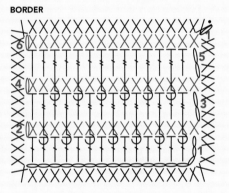

Fig. 3: Large Rag stitch pattern

Yarn Used

Nashua Handknits Ecologie Cotton, 100% natural dyed pima cotton, 1¾oz/50g = 110yd/101m per ball

Small Rag: 2 balls, Chestnut (#80)

Medium Rag: 2 balls, Indigo (#85)

Large Rag: 3 balls, Logwood (#86)

Stock Sweater

Every guy should have one of these in his wardrobe. Made in a neutral color, it goes with any shirt he has and will become the workhorse of his closet. I designed this version to be longer than usual to emphasize the comfort factor.

Instructions

Note: Sweater is worked as one piece.

1 x 1 Ribbing Pattern

Ch required number of sts.

Row 1: Dc in 4th ch from hook and in ea ch across, turn.

Row 2: Ch 2 (counts as hdc), *FPdc around the post of next st, BPdc around the post of next st; rep from * across to within last 2 sts, FPdc around the post of next st, hdc in last st, turn.

Row 3: Ch 2 (counts as hdc), *BPdc around the post of next st, FPdc around the post of next st; rep from * across to within last 2 sts, BPdc around the post of next st, hdc in last st, turn.

Rep rows 2–3 for pattern.

Pattern Stitch

Row 1: Ch 4, sk next st, *dc in next st, ch 1, sk next st; rep from * across to within last st, dc in last st, turn.

Row 2: Ch 3 (counts as dc), *working over ch-1 sp, tr in next skipped st 2 rows below, dc in next dc in current row; rep from * across, ending with a dc in last st. Rep rows 1–2 for pattern.

Skill Level
Beginner

Finished Size
Sizes: S (M, L, XL, XXL): 39 (40½, 42½, 44½, 47)"/99 (103, 108, 113, 119.5)cm
Sweater shown in size L.

You Will Need
678 (767, 861, 900, 1002)yd/620 (702, 788, 823, 917)m of **5** bulky weight yarn, in gray
Hook: 6.00mm (size J-10 U.S.) (*or size to obtain gauge*)
Yarn needle
Stitch markers

Stitches Used
Back post double crochet (BPdc)
Chain stitch (ch)
Double crochet (dc)
Front post double crochet (FPdc)
Slip stitch (sl st)
Treble crochet (tr)

Special Stitch
Double crochet two together (dc2tog): (Yo, insert hook in next st, yo, draw yarn through st, yo, draw yarn through 2 lps on hk) twice, yo, draw yarn through 3 lps on hook.
Double crochet three together (dc3tog): (Yo, insert hook in next st, yo, draw yarn through st, yo, draw yarn through 2 lps on hk) 3 times, yo, draw yarn through 4 lps on hook.

Gauge
11 sts x 9 rows = 4"/10cm in pattern stitch
Always take time to check your gauge.

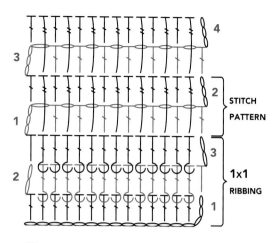

Fig. 1: Stitch and ribbing pattern

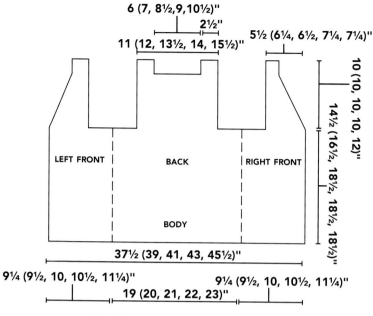

Fig. 2: Front and back diagram

Body

Ch 105 (109, 115, 121, 127).

Work in 1 x 1 ribbing pattern through row 2—103 (107, 113, 119, 125) sts.

Work even in pattern stitch until piece measures 14½ (16½, 18½, 18½, 18½)"/37 (42, 47, 47, 47)cm from beg, ending with a RS row.

Left Front

Work in pattern stitch across first 16 (17, 18, 20, 20) sts, turn.

SHAPE NECKLINE

Work in pattern stitch, dec 1 st (dc2tog) at neck edge at end of next row and every other row 6 (7, 6, 6, 6) times; then dec 2 sts (dc3tog) at neck edge at end of next row and every other row 0 (0, 1, 2, 2) times—7 sts at end of last row. Work even in pattern stitch

until piece measures 24½ (26½, 28½, 28½, 30½)"/62 (67.5, 72.5, 72.5, 77.5)cm from beg. Fasten off.

Back

Next row: With WS facing, sk 20 sts to the left of last made in first row of left front, join yarn in next st, starting in same st, work even in pattern stitch across next 31 (33, 37, 39, 43) sts, turn.

Work even until piece measures 5 rows less then finished left front.

SHAPE FIRST SHOULDER

Next row: Work in pattern stitch across first 6 sts, turn leaving rem sts unworked. Work even in pattern stitch for 4 more rows. Fasten off.

SHAPE SECOND SHOULDER

Next row: With WS facing, sk 17 (19, 23, 25, 29) sts to the left of last made in first row of first shoulder, join yarn in next st, starting in same st, work even in pattern stitch across, turn—7 sts.

Work even in pattern stitch for 4 more rows. Fasten off.

Right Front

Next row: With WS facing, sk 20 sts to the left of last made in first row of back, join yarn in next st, starting in same st, work even in pattern stitch across, turn—16 (17, 18, 20, 20) sts. Work same as left front, reversing shaping.

Assemble

Sew shoulder seams.

Finishing

ARMHOLE EDGING

Rnd 1 (RS): With RS facing, join yarn at center bottom of armhole, ch 3 (counts as dc), dc evenly around, working an even number of sts, sl st in 3rd ch of beg ch-3 to join, turn.

Rnd 2: Ch 2 (counts as hdc), *FPdc around the post of next st, BPdc around the post of next st; rep from * around to within last st, FPdc around the post of last st, sl st in 2nd ch of beg ch-2 to join, turn.

Rnd 3: Ch 2, *FPdc around the post of next FPdc, sk next BPdc; rep from * around to within last st, FPdc around the post of last st, sl st in 2nd ch of beg ch-2 to join. Fasten off.

SWEATER EDGING

Row 1: With RS facing, join yarn at bottom right-hand corner of right front, ch 3, dc evenly across right front edge, across back neck edge, and down left front edge to bottom left-hand corner of left front, working an odd number of sts, turn. Place 5 markers for buttonholes on left front edge, placing 1st marker 1"/2.5cm above bottom edge and ea rem marker 4"/10cm above last marker.

Row 2: Ch 2 (counts as hdc), working ch 1, sk next BPdc at ea marker for buttonholes, work *FPdc around the post of next st, BPdc around the post of next st; rep from * across, to within last 2 sts, FPdc around the post of next st, hdc in last st, turn.

Row 3: Ch 2 (counts as hdc), working hdc in ea ch-1 buttonhole sp, work *BPdc around the post of next st, FPdc around the post of next st; rep from * across to within buttonholes. last 2 sts, BPdc around the post of next st, hdc in last st, turn.

Row 4: Ch 2 (counts as hdc), *FPdc around the post of next st, BPdc around the post of next st; rep from * across to within last 2 sts, FPdc around the post of next st, hdc in last st, turn. Fasten off. Sew buttons on right front button band to correspond with buttonholes. Weave in ends.

Yarn Used

Patons Shetland Chunky Tweeds, 72% acrylic/25% wool/3% viscose, 3oz/85g = 108yd/99m per skein

7 (8, 8, 9, 10) skeins, Oxford Gray (#67046)

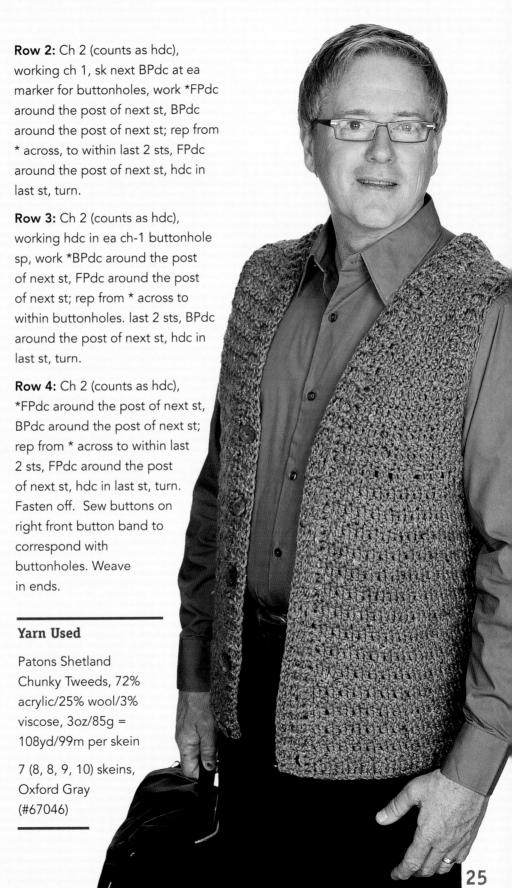

Boy Belt

As I was looking for the perfect fiber for this project, a little voice in my head kept saying "use yarn." While I usually listen to those voices, this time I decided to create this crocheted belt from shoestring-weight suede.

Instructions

Belt

Ch 5.

Row 1: Sc in 2nd ch from hook and in each ch across, turn—4 sc.

Rows 2–4: Ch 1, sc in each st across, turn—4 sc.

Row 5: Ch 2 (counts as dc), dc in BL only of ea st across, turn—4 dc.

Rep row 5 until belt measures 42"/106.5cm or to desired length.

Last row: Ch 1, working in BL only, sc in first st, hdc in next 2 sts, sc in last st. Fasten off.

Assemble

Use first 3 rows to wrap around center of belt buckle, and whipstitch into place. Weave in ends.

Yarn Used

Tejas Lace Company Genuine Suede ⅛"/3mm Lace, 100% suede, 25yd/23m per spool

2 spools, Lt. Rust (#5014-05)

Skill Level
Beginner

Finished Size
1¾ x 42"/4.5 x 106.5cm, adjustable to fit any waist

You Will Need
50yd/46m of ⅛"/3mm-wide suede lace, in brown
Hook: 6.50mm (size K-10½ U.S.) (*or size to obtain gauge*)
Yarn needle
1⅝"/4cm belt buckle

Stitches Used
Chain stitch (ch)
Double crochet (dc)
Single crochet (sc)
Slip stitch (sl st)

Gauge
Approx 9 sts x 4 rows = 4"/10cm in dc in BL only
Always take time to check your gauge.

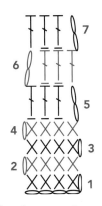

Fig. 1: Boy Belt pattern

Paw Warmers

Now that I have these slippers, I tell my well-meaning family to please not give me any more novelty slippers that look like dogs or beer steins or cartoon characters. I can whip up a pair of these in an evening and not scare the cats as I walk across the room.

Instructions

Slipper (make 2)

FOOT

Leaving a long tail, ch 24, and without twisting ch, sl st in first ch to form a ring.

Rnd 1: Sc in each ch around, do not join—24 sc. Work in a spiral. Place marker at beg of rnd and move marker up as work progresses.

Rnds 2–15 (WS): Hdc in FL only of each st around.

Note: You can modify the slipper length, if needed. If 15 rnds do not equal the length of your foot from the toe to the instep, add more rounds. Make it shorter by working fewer rounds.

ANKLE

Rnd 16: Work 12 chainless hdc, skip next 12 sts, hdc in FL only of next 12 sts.

Note: If you have a high instep, you can work more than 12 chainless hdc to accommodate your size, but don't skip more than 12 sts when you continue the rnd.

Continue to work in a spiral, moving marker up each rnd.

Skill Level
Intermediate

Finished Size
12"/30.5cm long x 8½"/21.5cm high at ankle—one size fits shoe sizes 9–11 (The instructions provide an option to modify the size for larger or smaller feet.)

You Will Need
170yd/156m of (6) super bulky weight yarn
Hook: 10.00mm (size N-15 U.S.) (*or size to obtain gauge*)
Stitch marker
Yarn needle

Stitches Used

Chain stitch (ch)
Half double crochet (hdc)
Single crochet (sc)
Slip stitch (sl st)

Special Stitches

Chainless hdc: Insert hook in last st made, yo, pull up loop, yo, pull through first loop on hook to create a ch, yo, pull through two loops on hook. *Hint: if you pinch the ch created inside the st, it is easier to create the next st.* Yo, insert hook in ch that you are pinching, yo, pull up loop, yo, pull through first loop on hook to create a ch, yo, pull through three loops on hook. Continue as established until indicated number of chainless hdc are made.

Single crochet two together (sc2tog): (Insert hook in next st, yo, draw yarn through st) twice, yo, draw yarn through 3 lps on hook.

Gauge

12 sts x 6 rows = 4"/10cm in hdc in FL only
Always take time to check your gauge.

Rnds 17–24: Hdc in FL only in each st around. At end of rnd 24, sl st in next hdc to join. Fasten off.

HEEL

Rnd 1: Locate center of rem sts in rnd 15 of Foot. With RS facing, join yarn with a sc in BL of next st in rnd 15 of Foot, working in BL of sts, sc in ea st across to within last st on Foot, sc2tog worked across next st on Foot and first st on lower edge of Ankle, sc in ea st across to within last st on lower edge of Ankle, sc2tog in next st of Ankle and next st of Foot, sc in ea st around to beg, do not join. Work in a spiral as before.

Rnd 2: *Sc in each sc across to next sc2tog, sc2tog in next 2 sts; rep from * once, sc in ea st around to beg, do not join.

Rep rnd 2, dec 2 sts ea rnd until 10 sts remain. At end of last rnd, sl st in next sc to join. Fasten off, leaving a sewing length.

Finishing

Turn slipper inside out. To close toe, use tail to weave in and out of foundation ch. Gather tightly and secure. Flatten heel lengthwise and whipstitch seam. Weave in all ends. Turn RS out, put on feet, and chase cat around room.

Yarn Used

Patons Shetland Chunky Tweeds, 75% acrylic/25% wool, 3oz/85g = 108yd/99m per skein

2 skeins, Medium Blue (#67108)

Baffy Buddies

The baffy might be the least used of the woods in your golf bag, but isn't that all the more reason to protect it with a great-looking cover? These protectors are designed to fit all your woods, so make as many as you need.

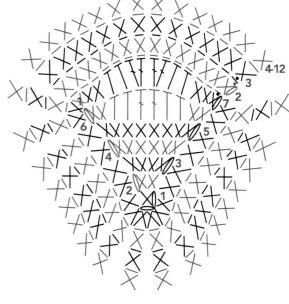

Fig. 1: Top, and rounds 1–12 of sides

Skill Level
Beginner

Finished Size
One size fits most golf club woods:
  11"/28cm in circumference x
  9"/23cm tall

You Will Need
 Color A: 143yd/131m of super
  bulky weight yarn, in tan
Color B: 100yd/ 92m of super
  bulky weight yarn, in multi-color
  variegated
Hook: 6.50mm (size K-10½ U.S.) (or
  size to obtain gauge)
Stitch marker
Yarn needle
Golf clubs (optional)

Stitches Used
Chain stitch (ch)
Double crochet (dc)
Half double crochet (hdc)
Single crochet (sc)
Slip stitch (sl st)

Gauge
11 sts x 10 rows = 4"/10cm sc
*Always take time to check your
  gauge.*

Instructions

Top

With B, ch 2.

Row 1: Sc in 2nd ch from hook, turn—1 sc.

Row 2: Ch 1, 2 sc in next sc, turn—2 sc.

Row 3: Ch 1, 2 sc in ea sc across, turn—4 sc.

Row 4: Ch 1, 2 sc in first sc, sc in next 2 sc, 2 sc in last sc, turn—6 sc.

Row 5: Ch 1, 2 sc in first sc, sc in next 4 sc, 2 sc in last sc, turn—8 sc.

Row 6: Ch 1, 2 sc in first sc, hdc in next 2 sc, dc in next 2 sc, hdc in next 2 sc, 2 sc in last sc, turn—10 sts.

Row 7: Ch 1, 2 sc in first st, sc in next st, hdc in next 2 sts, 2 dc in next 2 sts, hdc in next 2 sts, sc in next st, 2 sc in last st, do not turn—14 sts.

Sides

Rnd 1: Work 1 more sc in same st, working through the ends of the rows, sc evenly down side of Top, work 4 sc in foundation ch, working through the ends of the rows, sc evenly up side of Top to beginning of row 7, work 1 more sc in first st of row 7, sl st in first sc to join.

Rnd 2: Ch 1, sc in BL only of ea st around, sl st in first sc to join—32 sc. Fasten off.

Rnd 3: Join A with sc in BL of any st, sc in BL only of ea st around, do not join. Work in a spiral. Place marker at beg of rnd, and move marker up as work progresses.

Rnds 4–12: Sc in BL only of ea st around. At end of rnd 12, sl st in next sc to join. Fasten off.

Rnd 13: With RS facing, join Color B with a sl st to BL of any st, ch 3 (counts as dc), dc in BL only of ea st around, join with a sl st to top of beginning ch-3—32 dc.

Rnd 14: Working through both lps of sts, ch 3 (counts as dc), dc in ea st around, join with a sl st to top of beginning ch-3.

Rnd 15: Ch 4, skip next dc, *dc in next dc, ch 1, skip next dc; rep from * around, sl st to 3rd ch of beginning ch-4 to join.

Rnd 16: Ch 3 (counts as dc), dc in ea dc and ea ch-1 space around, sl st to top of beginning ch-3 to join. Fasten off.

Drawstring

With Color A, ch 61, sl st in 2nd ch from hook and in ea ch across. Fasten off.

Assemble

Weave drawstring in and out of spaces created in rnd 15, tie ea end of drawstring in an overhand knot. Weave in ends.

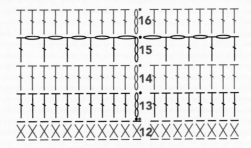

Fig. 2: Rounds 12–16 of sides

Yarn Used

Red Heart Grande, 100% acrylic, 6oz/170g = 143yd/130m per skein

(A) 1 skein, Linen (#2332)

(B) 1 skein, Polo Multi (#2920)

Saugatuck Winter

I spent my youth in Saugatuck, Michigan, where we knew that the only colder place in the country in wintertime was Nome, Alaska . . . maybe. I had a sweater just like this one, and it was my absolute favorite for comfort and style.

Instructions

1 x 1 Ribbing Pattern

Ch required number of sts.

Row 1: Dc in 4th ch from hook and in ea ch across, turn.

Row 2: Ch 2 (counts as hdc), *FPdc around the post of next st, BPdc around the post of next st; rep from * across to within last st, hdc in last st, turn.

Rep row 2 for pattern.

STITCH PATTERN

Row 1: Ch 1, sc in first st, dc in next st, *sc in next st, dc in next st; rep from * across, turn.

Row 2: Ch 3 (counts as dc), sc in next dc, *dc in next sc, sc in next dc; rep from * across, turn.

Rep row 2 for stitch pattern.

Skill Level
Intermediate

Finished Size
S (M, L, XL, XXL): 40 (42, 44, 46, 48)"/101.5 (106.5, 112, 117, 122)cm
Sweater shown in size XL.

You Will Need
1296 (1404, 1512, 1620, 1836)yd/1185 (1284, 1383, 1482, 1679)m of (**6**) super bulky weight yarn, in light blue tweed
Hook: 10.00mm (size N-15 U.S.) (*or size to obtain gauge*)
Yarn needle

Stitches Used
Back post double crochet (BPdc)
Chain stitch (ch)
Double crochet (dc)
Front post double crochet (FPdc)
Single crochet (sc)
Slip stitch (sl st)

Special Stitch
Single crochet two together (sc2tog): (Insert hook in next st, yo, draw yarn through st) twice, yo, draw yarn through 3 lps on hk.

Gauge
11 sts x 8 rows = 4"/10cm in stitch pattern
Always take time to check your gauge.

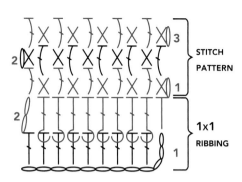

Fig. 1: Stitch and ribbing pattern

STITCH PATTERN

1x1 RIBBING

Back

Ch 56 (60, 62, 64, 68).

Work in 1 x 1 ribbing pattern through row 2—54 (58, 60, 62, 66) sts.

Work even in stitch pattern until piece measures 15 (15½, 16, 16, 17)"/38 (39.5, 40.5, 40.5, 43)cm from beg.

SHAPE ARMHOLES

Next row: *Sl st in ea of first 3 sts, starting in same st, work in stitch pattern across to within last 2 sts, turn, leaving rem sts unworked—50 (54, 56, 58, 62) sts.

Rep last row 2 more times—42 (46, 48, 50, 54) sts at end of last row.

Cont in stitch pattern until piece measures 23 (23½, 25, 25, 27)"/58.5 (59.5, 63.5, 63.5, 68.5)cm from beg.

SHAPE FIRST SHOULDER

Next row: Work in stitch pattern across first 14 (15, 15, 16, 16) sts, turn, leaving rem sts unworked.

Next row: Work in stitch pattern across. Fasten off.

SHAPE SECOND SHOULDER

Next row: Sk 14 (16, 18, 18, 22) sts to the left of last st made in first row of first shoulder, join yarn in next st, starting in same st, work in stitch pattern across, turn—14 (15, 15, 16, 16) sts.

Next row: Work in stitch pattern across. Fasten off.

Front

Work same as back through armholes.

SHAPE FIRST SHOULDER

Next row: Work in stitch pattern across first 14 (15, 15, 16, 16) sts, turn, leaving rem sts unworked.

Work even in stitch pattern until piece measures same as finished back. Fasten off.

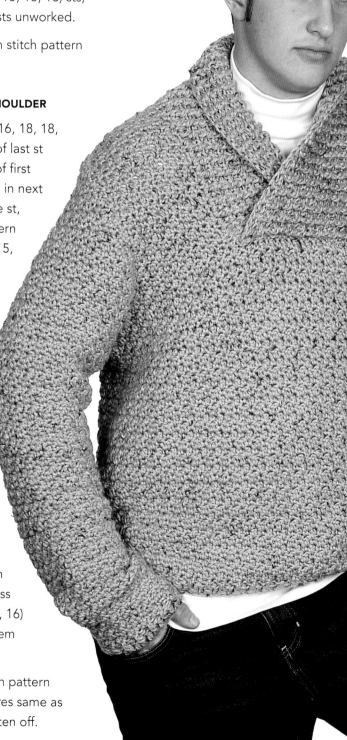

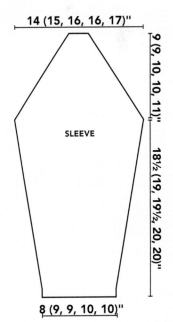

SHAPE SECOND SHOULDER

Next row: Sk 14 (16, 18, 18, 22) sts to the left of last st made in first row of first shoulder, join yarn in next st, starting in same st, work in stitch pattern across, turn—14 (15, 15, 16, 16) sts.

Work even in stitch pattern until piece measures same as finished back. Fasten off.

Sleeve (make 2)

Ch 24 (26, 26, 30, 30).

Work in 1 x 1 ribbing pattern through row 2—22 (24, 24, 28, 28) sts.

Work in stitch pattern, inc 1 st at beg and end of next row and every 5 (4, 4, 5, 5) rows until 38 (42, 44, 44, 46) sts are on work, then work even until sleeve measures 18½ (19, 19½, 20, 20)"/47 (48.5, 49.5, 51, 51)cm from beg.

SHAPE SLEEVE CAP

Work in stitch pattern, dec 1 st at the end of ea of next 3 (0, 1, 1, 2) rows, then dec 1 st at the beg and end of next 15 (18, 19, 19, 20) rows. Fasten off.

Assemble

Sew shoulder seams. Set in sleeves. Sew sleeve and side seams.

Finishing

COLLAR

With RS facing, join yarn with a sl st to end st of first row of neckline on right side, ch 3 (counts as dc), dc evenly up side of neckline, across back neck edge, and down the left side of neckline, working an even number of sts, turn.

Work in 1 x 1 ribbing pattern, repeating row 2 until collar measures 5 (6, 7, 7, 8)"/12.5 (15, 18, 18, 20.5)cm from beg. Fasten off.

With left side of collar overlapping right side of collar, sew sides of collar to front of sweater at base of neckline.

Weave in ends.

Yarn Used

Patons Shetland Chunky Tweeds, 72% acrylic/25% wool/3% viscose, 3oz/85g = 108yd/99m per skein

12 (13, 14, 15, 17) skeins, Sea Ice (#67128)

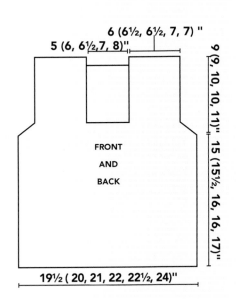

6 (6½, 6½, 7, 7)"
5 (6, 6½, 7, 8)"

FRONT
AND
BACK

9 (9, 10, 10, 11)"
15 (15½, 16, 16, 17)"

19½ (20, 21, 22, 22½, 24)"

Fig. 2: Front and back diagram

14 (15, 16, 16, 17)"

SLEEVE

9 (9, 10, 10, 11)"
18½ (19, 19½, 20, 20)"

8 (9, 9, 10, 10)"

Fig. 3: Sleeve diagram

Free Digits

I tried to cut the fingers off my gloves once when I was in a marching band so I could finger my sax easier, but the gloves unraveled and ended up around my wrists. With this crochet version, I can chop wood, haul brush, or ride my hog without losing my grip. Well, if I had a hog.

Instructions

Glove (make 2)

Ch 30.

Row 1 (WS): Hdc into 3rd ch from hook and in each ch across, turn—29 hdc.

Row 2 (RS): Ch 1, sc in BL of each st across, turn—29 sc.

Row 3: Ch 1, hdc in each sc across, turn—29 hdc.

Rows 4–19: Rep rows 2–3.

Row 20: Rep row 2.

Fasten off.

Assemble

With RS facing, fold glove lengthwise. Matching sts, sew last row to foundation ch across first 1½"/4cm from one end, skip 2½"/6.5cm for thumbhole, sew remainder of seam to other end of glove. Turn glove RS out.

Thumb

Rnd 1: With RS facing, join yarn with sl st to bottom of thumb opening, ch 1, sc evenly around opening, sl st in first sc to join, turn.

Rnd 2: Ch 2 (counts as hdc), hdc in each st around, sl st in top of beg ch-2 to join, turn.

Rnd 3: Ch 1, *sc in BL of next st, skip next st; rep from * around, sl st to top of first sc to join. Fasten off.

Weave in ends.

Skill Level
Beginner

Finished Size
10"/25.5cm long x 8"/20.5cm in circumference—one size fits most hands.

You Will Need
140yd/128m of (**5**) bulky weight yarn
Hook: 6.00mm (size J-10 U.S.) (*or size to obtain gauge*)
Yarn needle

Stitches Used
Chain stitch (ch)
Half double crochet (hdc)
Single crochet (sc)
Slip stitch (sl st)

Gauge
11 sts x 10 rows = 4"/10cm in sc
Always take time to check your gauge.

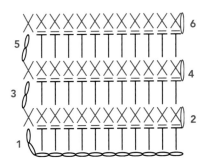

Fig. 1: Stitch pattern

Yarn Used

Red Heart Casual Cot'n Blend, 61% acrylic/29% cotton/10% polyester, 4oz/113g = 140yd/128m per skein

1 skein, Parsley (#3642)

Dawg

Who knew that a hoodie would become a timeless classic? I've always had a hooded sweatshirt or two in my closet, so I wanted to design a crochet version. The soft and comfy fiber used here creates a denim look.

Instructions

Pattern Stitch

Row 1: Sc in 2nd ch from hook, dc in next ch, *sc in next ch, dc in next ch; rep from * across, turn.

Row 2: Ch 3 (counts as dc), sc in next sc, *dc in next dc, sc in next sc; rep from * across, turn.

Row 3: Ch 1, sc in same first sc, dc in next dc, *sc in next sc, dc in next dc; rep from * across, turn.

Repeat rows 2–3 for pattern.

Back

Ch 65 (67, 71, 73, 77).

Work even in pattern stitch on 64 (66, 70, 72, 76) sts until piece measures 15 (15½, 16, 16, 16½)"/38 (39.5, 40.5, 40.5, 42)cm from beg.

Skill Level
Intermediate

Finished Size
S (M, L, XL, XXL): 42 (44, 46, 48, 50)"/106.5 (112, 117, 122, 127)cm
Sweater shown in size M.

You Will Need
1673 (1725, 1935, 2091, 2196)yd/1530 (1578, 1770, 1912, 2008)m of (**4**) medium weight yarn
Hook: 5.00mm (size H-8 U.S.) (*or size to obtain gauge*)
Yarn needle
Long sewing pins
Stitch marker

Stitches Used
Back post double crochet (BPdc)
Chain stitch (ch)
Double crochet (dc)
Front post double crochet (FPdc)
Single crochet (sc)
Slip stitch (sl st)

Gauge
12 sts x 10 rows = 4"/10cm in pattern stitch
Always take time to check your gauge.

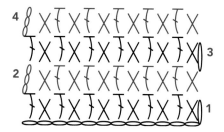

Fig. 1: Pattern stitch

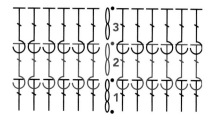

Fig. 2: Bottom ribbing and cuffs pattern

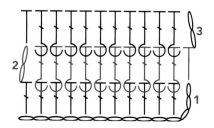

Fig. 3: Hood ribbing pattern

SHAPE ARMHOLES

Next row: Work in established pattern across to within last 8 sts, turn, leaving rem sts unworked—56 (58, 62, 64, 68) sts.

Next row: Rep last row—48 (50, 54, 56, 60) sts.

Work even in pattern until piece measures 24 (25, 26, 26½, 27½)"/61 (63.5, 66, 67.5, 70)cm from beg.

Fasten off.

Front

Work as for back including armhole shaping until piece measures 22 (23, 24, 24½, 25½)"/56 (58.5, 61, 62, 65)cm from beg.

SHAPE FIRST SHOULDER

Next row: Work in pattern across first 16 (16, 16, 18, 18) sts, turn, leaving rem sts unworked—16 (16, 16, 18, 18) sts.

Work even until piece measures 24 (25, 26, 26½, 27½)"/61 (63.5, 66, 67.5, 70)cm from beg. Fasten off.

SHAPE SECOND SHOULDER

Next row: Sk 15 (18, 22, 20, 24) sts to the left of last st made in first row of first shoulder, join yarn in next st, work in established pattern across, turn—16 (16, 16, 18, 18) sts.

Work even in pattern until piece measures 24 (25, 26, 26½, 27½)"/61 (63.5, 66, 67.5, 70)cm from beg. Fasten off.

Sleeve (make 2)

Ch 23 (23, 29, 31, 31).

Work even in pattern stitch for 4 rows—22 (22, 28, 30, 30) sts. Maintaining pattern stitch, inc 1 st in pattern at end of each row until 53 (57, 59, 63, 65) sts are on work. Work even until length of sleeve measures 24 (25½, 26, 26½, 27)"/61 (65, 66, 67.5, 68.5)cm from beg.

Pocket

Ch 41.

Rows 1–8: Work even in pattern stitch, turn—40 sts.

Rows 9–12: Work in pattern stitch across to within 2 sts, turn, leaving rem sts unworked—32 sts at end of last row.

Rows 13–21: Work even in pattern stitch, turn. Fasten off.

EDGING

Rnd 1: Ch 1, sc evenly around entire pocket, sl st in first sc to join. Fasten off.

Drawstring

Make a 60"/152.5cm long ch. Fasten off. Tie ea end of drawstring in an overhand knot.

Assemble

Sew shoulder seams. Set in sleeves. Sew sleeve and side seams. Center pocket on front of sweater, sew in place, leaving sides of rows 9–21 unattached.

Finishing

HOOD

Row 1: With RS facing, join yarn at center front of neck opening, work in row 1 of pattern stitch around entire neck opening, working a multiple of 4 sts. Do not join, turn.

Work even in pattern stitch until hood measures 12"/30.5cm from beg.

SHAPE FIRST SIDE

Place marker at center of last row

Row 1: Work even in pattern stitch across to within 2 sts of center marker, turn, leaving rem sts unworked.

Row 2: Work even in pattern stitch across, turn.

Row 3: Work even in pattern stitch across to within last 2 sts, turn, leaving rem sts unworked.

Row 4: Work even in pattern stitch across, turn. Fasten off.

SHAPE SECOND SIDE

Row 1: Sk 2 sts to the left of center marker, work in pattern stitch across, turn.

Row 2: Work even in pattern stitch across, turn.

Row 3: Sl st in first 3 sts, work in pattern stitch across, turn.

Row 4: Work even in pattern stitch across, turn. Fasten off.

BOTTOM RIBBING

Rnd 1: With RS facing, join yarn on bottom edge at one side seam, ch 3 (counts as dc), dc evenly around, working an even number of sts.

Rnd 2: Ch 2 (counts as hdc), *BPdc around the post of next dc, FPdc around the post of next dc; rep from * around, ending with BPdc around the post of last dc, sl st in 2nd ch of beg ch-2 to join.

Rnd 3: Rep rnd 2. Fasten off.

CUFFS

Rnd 1: With RS facing, join yarn on cuff edge of one sleeve, at seam, ch 3 (counts as dc), dc evenly around, working an even number of sts.

Rnds 2–3: Rep rnds 2–3 of bottom ribbing. Fasten off.

Rep cuff on other sleeve.

HOOD RIBBING

Row 1: With RS facing, join yarn at lower right-hand corner of hood edge, ch 3 (counts as dc), dc evenly across to lower left-hand corner, working an even number of sts.

Row 2: Ch 2 (counts as hdc), *BPdc around the post of next dc, FPdc around the post of next dc; rep from * across, ending with hdc in top of ch-3 tch, turn.

Row 3: Rep row 2. Fasten off.

Weave in ends.

Yarn Used

Moda Dea Fashionista, 50% acrylic/50% tencel lyocell, 3½oz/100g = 183yd/168m per skein

10 (10, 11, 12, 12) skeins, Blue Jean (#6130)

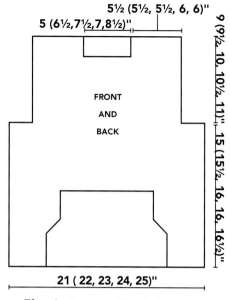

5½ (5½, 5½, 6, 6)"

5 (6½,7½,7,8½)"

9 (9½, 10, 10½, 11)", 15 (15½, 16, 16, 16½)"

FRONT AND BACK

21 (22, 23, 24, 25)"

Fig. 4: Front and back diagram

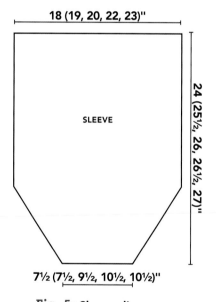

18 (19, 20, 22, 23)"

24 (25½, 26, 26½, 27)"

SLEEVE

7½ (7½, 9½, 10½, 10½)"

Fig. 5: Sleeve diagram

Comforolled

Some guys don't like the ribbing on most sweaters. That's why I've created this sweater that has a rolled hem instead of ribbing. The entire sweater is worked up in single crochet, so this is a great project for beginners.

Skill Level
Intermediate

Finished Size
S (M, L, XL, XXL): 38 (40, 42, 44, 46)"/96.5 (101.5, 106.5, 112, 117)cm
Sweater shown in size XL.

You Will Need
1404 (1538, 1680, 1800, 1976)yd/1284 (1407, 1536, 1646, 1807)m of (**4**) medium weight yarn, in green
Hook: 5.00mm (size H-8 U.S.) (*or size to obtain gauge*)
Long sewing pins
Yarn needle

Stitches Used
Chain stitch (ch)
Single crochet (sc)
Slip stitch (sl st)

Special Stitch
Single crochet two together (sc2tog): (Insert hook in next st, yo, draw yarn through st) twice, yo, draw yarn through 3 lps on hook.

Gauge
17 sts x 17 rows = 4"/10cm in sc
Always take time to check your gauge.

Instructions

Rolled Hem

Row 1 (RS): Sc in FL of 2nd ch from hook, sc in FL of ea ch across, turn.

Row 2: Ch 1, sc in BL only of each sc across, turn.

Row 3: Ch 1, sc in FL only of each sc across, turn.

Rows 4–5: Rep rows 2–3.

Row 6: Rep row 2.

Back

Ch 82 (86, 90, 95, 99).

Row 1 (RS): Sc in FL of 2nd ch from hook, sc in FL of ea ch across, turn—81 (85, 89, 94, 98) sc.

Rows 2–6: Work rows 2–6 of Rolled Hem pattern.

Working in both lps of sts, work even in sc until piece measures 15 (15½, 16, 16, 16½)"/38 (39.5, 40.5, 40.5, 42)cm from beg.

SHAPE ARMHOLES

Next Row: Ch 1, sc in each sc across to within last 9 sts, turn, leaving rem sts unworked—72 (76, 80, 85, 89) sc.

Next row: Rep last row—63 (67, 71, 76, 80) sc.

Work even in sc until piece measures 23 (24, 25, 25½, 26½)"/58.5 (61, 63.5, 65, 67.5)cm from beg.

SHAPE FIRST SHOULDER

Next row: Ch 1, sc in each of next 16 (18, 20, 22, 24) sc, turn, leaving rem sts unworked—16 (18, 20, 22, 24) sc.

Work even in sc until piece measures 24 (25, 26, 26½, 27½)"/61 (63.5, 66, 67.5, 70)cm from beg. Fasten off.

SHAPE SECOND SHOULDER

Next row: Sk 31 (31, 31, 32, 32) sts to the left of last st made in first row of First Shoulder, join yarn in next sc, ch 1, sc in ea sc across—16 (18, 20, 22, 24) sc.

Work even in sc until piece measures 24 (25, 26, 26½, 27½)"/61 (63.5, 66, 67.5, 70)cm from beg. Fasten off.

Front

Work as for back including armhole shaping until piece measures 21 (22, 23, 23½, 24½)"/53.5 (56, 58.5, 59.5, 62)cm from beg. Shape shoulders same as back.

Sleeves (make 2)

Row 1 (RS): Sc in FL of 2nd ch from hook, sc in FL of ea ch across, turn—34 (38, 43, 43, 47) sc.

Rows 2–6: Work rows 2–6 of Rolled Hem pattern.

Working in both lps of sts, work in sc, inc 1 sc at beg and end of every 3rd row until 64 (68, 73, 77, 85) sc are on work. Work even in sc until Sleeve measures 18½ (19, 19½, 20, 20½)"/47 (48.5, 49.5, 51, 52)cm from beg.

SHAPE SLEEVE CAP

Continue in sc, dec 1 st at end of each row 31 (31, 31, 30, 26) times. Dec 1 st at beg and end of each row 14 (16, 18, 21, 27) times. Fasten off.

Assemble

Sew shoulder seams. Set in sleeves. Sew sleeve and side seams.

Finishing

COLLAR

Foundation rnd: With WS facing, join yarn at center back of neck, ch 1, sc evenly around, sl st in first sc to join, turn.

Rnd 1 (RS): Ch 1, sc in FL of ea sc around, sl st in FL of first sc to join, turn.

Rnd 2: Ch 1, sc in BL of ea sc around, sl st in BL of first sc to join, turn.

Rnd 3: Ch 1, sc in FL of ea sc around, sl st in FL of first sc to join, turn.

Rnds 4–9: Rep rnds 2–3.

Rnd 10: Rep rnd 2. Fasten off. Weave in ends.

Yarn Used

Patons Décor, 75% acrylic/25% wool, 3½oz/100g = 210yd/193m per skein

7 (8, 8, 9, 10) skeins, New Green (#16523)

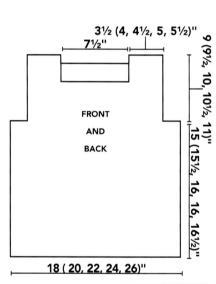

3½ (4, 4½, 5, 5½)"

7½"

FRONT
AND
BACK

9 (9½, 10, 10½, 11)"

15 (15½, 16, 16, 16½)"

18 (20, 22, 24, 26)"

Fig. 1: Front and back diagram

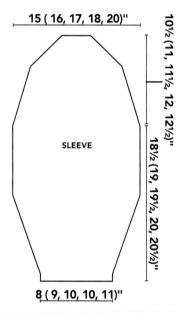

15 (16, 17, 18, 20)"

10½ (11, 11½, 12, 12½)"

SLEEVE

18½ (19, 19½, 20, 20½)"

8 (9, 10, 10, 11)"

Fig. 2: Sleeve diagram

Calvarium Skullcap

A buddy of mine was a skateboarder. I didn't get why he wanted to break his bones defying the laws of gravity, but I did like the cool hats he wore. After two quick measurements, you can customize this pattern and use any yarn to make your own personal statement.

Skill Level
Beginner

Finished Size
8"/20.5cm deep x 23"/58.5cm in circumference—one size fits most adults.

You Will Need
Approx 84yd/77m of (5) bulky weight yarn
Hook: 6.50mm (size K-10½ U.S.) (*or size to obtain gauge*)
Tape measure
Yarn needle

Stitches Used
Chain stitch (ch)
Half double crochet (hdc)
Single crochet (sc)
Slip stitch (sl st)

Gauge
The gauge will vary depending on the yarn and hook you use. For the piece in the photo, I used a size K hook for each cap, but the number of stitches you'll need depends on the measurements you take (see instructions).
Always take time to check your gauge.

Yarn Used On Model's Hat

Patons Rumor, 84% acrylic/15% alpaca/1% polyester, 2.8oz/80g = 84yd/77m per skein

1 skein, Fern Heather (#69525)

Instructions

Using the tape measure, measure from the top of your head to just above your eyebrows and write the number next to "A" below. Now measure the circumference of your head, being sure to go over your ears, and write the number next to "B" below.

A: _____   B: _____

The pattern below reflects the measurements (in parentheses) I used to create the hats in the photo. They fit an average-sized man—not that I'm average. I'm actually special and so are you, and aren't you glad you're not my therapist?

Pattern Stitch

Make a ch the length of measurement A (8"/20.5cm to match sample).

Row 1 (RS): Sc in 2nd ch from hook and in each ch across, turn.

Row 2: Ch 2, hdc in FL of each st across, turn.

Row 3: Ch 1, sc in BL of each st across, turn.

Rep rows 2–3 until length of piece = measurement B (23"/58.5cm to match sample). Fasten off.

Assemble

With RS facing, whipstitch the short ends together to form a tube. Turn hat RS out. Weave a long length of yarn in and out of end stitches of one side of the tube, cinch tightly, and secure with a knot.

Finishing

Weave in ends. Put it on head and grab your board, bro!

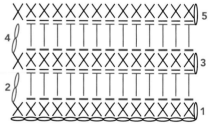

Fig. 1: Pattern stitch

To Aran Is Human

When I first became a designer, I decided to deconstruct some garments. I saw a way of recreating them in strips that would make it easy to modify the fit perfectly. This is the first time I've ever used this method on a man's garment. I love how it turned out!

Skill Level
Intermediate

Finished Size
S (M, L, XL, XXL): 39½ (42½, 45½, 47½, 50½)"/100.5 (108, 115.5, 120.5, 128.5)cm
Sweater shown in size XXL.

You Will Need
1784 (1976, 2231, 2323, 2457)yd/1632 (1807, 2040, 2124, 2247)m of ④ medium weight yarn, in cream
Hook: 5.00mm (size H-8 U.S.) (or size to obtain gauge)
Stitch markers
Yarn needle

Stitches Used
Back post double crochet (BPdc)
Chain stitch (ch)
Double crochet (dc)
Front post double crochet (FPdc)
Slip stitch (sl st)

Special Stitches
Each panel uses special stitches unique to that panel. See definitions for special stitches at the beginning of each panel instruction.

Gauge
15 sts x 8 rows = 4"/10cm in pattern stitch of Panel C
Always take time to check your gauge.

Instructions

Note: This sweater is worked up in panels or "strips," which you then whipstitch together. Feel free to lengthen or shorten the panels to fit your body type.

1 x 1 Ribbing Pattern

Row 1: Ch 3 (counts as dc), dc evenly across, turn.

Row 2: Ch 2 (counts as hdc), *FPdc around the post of next st, BPdc around the post of next st; rep from * across to within last st, hdc in last st, turn.

Panel A (make 2)

SPECIAL STITCHES

Front post treble crochet (FPtr): Yo (twice), insert hook from front to back to front again around the post of next designated st, yo, draw yarn though st, (yo, draw yarn through 2 loops on hk) 3 times, sk st behind FPtr just made.

Cable A (Cbl-A): Sk next 2 sts, FPtr around the post of next st, BPdc around the post of 2nd skipped st, FPtr around the post of 1st skipped st.

Cable B (Cbl-B): Sk next 2 sts, FPtr around the post of next st, BPdc around the post of 2nd skipped st, working under the front post just made, work FPtr around the post of 1st skipped st.

PATTERN STITCH

Ch 25 (25, 25, 29, 29).

Foundation row: Dc in 4th ch from hook and in each ch across, turn— 23 (23, 23, 27, 27) sts.

Row 1 (RS): Ch 2, BPdc around the post of next st, *Cbl-A across next 3 sts, BPdc around the post of next st; rep from * across, ending with hdc in last st, turn.

Fig. 1: 1 x 1 ribbing pattern

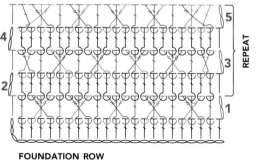

Fig. 2: Panel A pattern

FOUNDATION ROW

REPEAT

Row 2: Ch 2, FPdc around the post of every front raised st; BPdc around the post of every back raised st, hdc in last st, turn.

Row 3: Ch 2, sk next st, FPdc around the post of next st, BPdc around the post of last skipped st, BPdc around the post of next st, *Cbl-B across next 3 sts, BPdc around the post of next st; rep from * across to within last 3 sts, sk next st, BPdc around the post of next st, FPdc around the post of last skipped st, hdc in last st, turn.

Row 4: Rep row 2.

Row 5: Ch 2, sk next st, BPdc around the post of next st, sk one more st, FPtr around the post of next st, BPdc around the post of 2nd skipped st, FPtr around the post of 1st skipped st *BPdc around the post of next st, Cbl-A across next 3 sts; rep from * across to within last 5 sts, sk next 3 sts, FPtr around the post of next st, BPdc around the post of 2nd skipped st, FPtr around the post of 1st skipped st, BPdc around

the post of 3rd skipped st, hdc in last st, turn.

Rep rows 2–5 until panel measures 35½ (38, 40½, 40, 40)"/90 (96.5, 103, 101.5, 101.5)cm; place stitch markers at beg and end of row at 17 (19, 21, 20, 20)"/43 (48.5, 53.5, 51, 51)cm from beg.

Panel B (make 2)

SPECIAL STITCHES

Cable A (Cbl-A): Sk next st, FPdc around the post of next st, FPdc around the post of last skipped st.

Cable B (Cbl-B): Sk next st, BPdc around the post of next st, FPdc around the post of last skipped st.

Cable C (Cbl-C): Sk next st, FPdc around the post of next st, BPdc around the post of last skipped st.

Cable D (Cbl-D): Sk 2 sts, FPtr around the post of next st, BPdc around the post of 2nd skipped st, FPtr around the post of 1st skipped st.

PATTERN STITCH

Ch 26.

Foundation row: Dc in 4th ch from hook and in each ch across, turn—24 sts.

Row 1 (RS): Ch 2, BPdc in next 2 sts, Cbl-A, BPdc in next 2 sts, FPdc in next st, BPdc in next 11 sts, FPdc in next st, BPdc in next 3 sts, hdc in last st, turn.

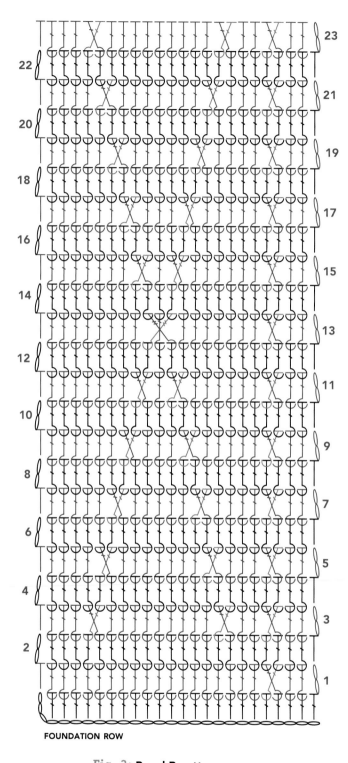

22
20
18
16
14
12
10
8
6
4
2

23
21
19
17
15
13
11
9
7
5
3
1

FOUNDATION ROW

Fig. 3: Panel B pattern

Row 2 and all even-numbered rows: Ch 2, FPdc around the post of every front raised st; BPdc around the post of every back raised st, hdc in last st, turn.

Row 3: Ch 2, BPdc in next 2 sts, Cbl-A, BPdc in next 2 sts, Cbl-B, BPdc in next 9 sts, Cbl-C, BPdc in next 3 sts, hdc in last st, turn.

Row 5: Ch 2, BPdc in next 2 sts, Cbl-A, BPdc in next 3 sts, Cbl-B, BPdc in next 7 sts, Cbl-C, BPdc in next 4 sts, hdc in last st, turn.

Row 7: Ch 2, BPdc in next 2 sts, Cbl-A, BPdc in next 4 sts, Cbl-B, BPdc in next 5 sts, Cbl-C, BPdc in next 5 sts, hdc in last st, turn.

Row 9: Ch 2, BPdc in next 2 sts, Cbl-A, BPdc in next 5 sts, Cbl-B, BPdc in next 3 sts, Cbl-C, BPdc in next 6 sts, hdc in last st, turn.

Row 11: Ch 2, BPdc in next 2 sts, Cbl-A, BPdc in next 6 sts, Cbl-B, BPdc in next st, Cbl-C, BPdc in next 7 sts, hdc in last st, turn.

Row 13: Ch 2, BPdc in next 2 sts, Cbl-A, BPdc in next 7 sts, Cbl-D, BPdc in next 8 sts, hdc in last st.

Row 15: Ch 2, BPdc in next 2 sts, Cbl-A, BPdc in next 6 sts, Cbl-C, BPdc in next st, Cbl-B, BPdc in next 7 sts, hdc in last st, turn.

Row 17: Ch 2, BPdc in next 2 sts, Cbl-A, BPdc in next 5 sts, Cbl-C, BPdc in next 3 sts, Cbl-B, BPdc in next 6 sts, hdc in last st, turn.

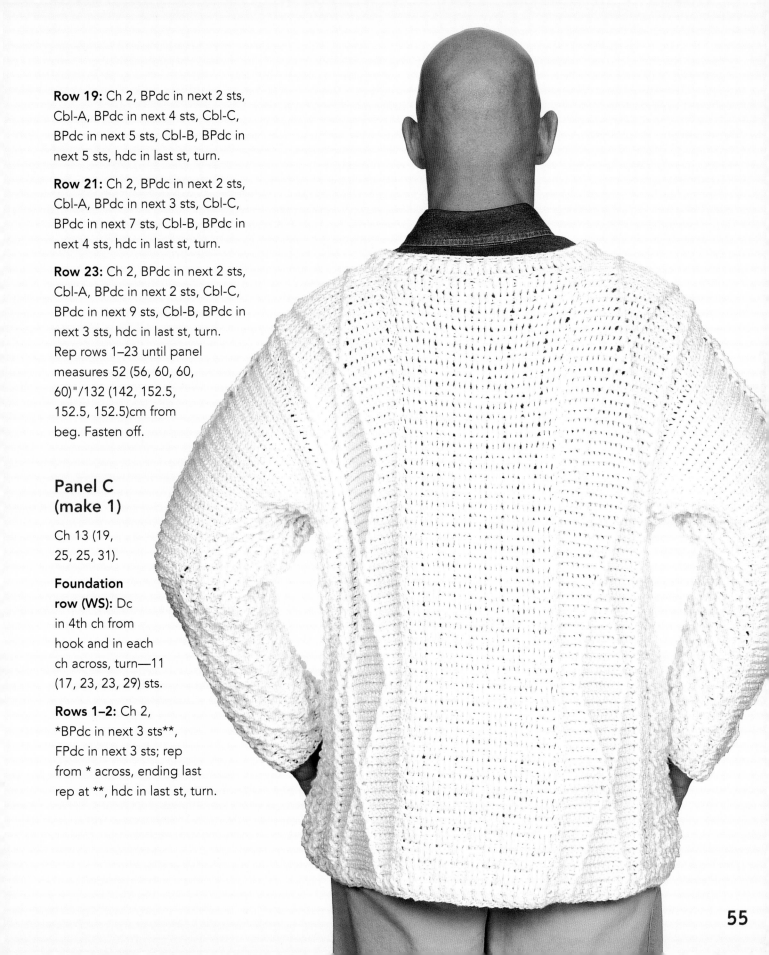

Row 19: Ch 2, BPdc in next 2 sts, Cbl-A, BPdc in next 4 sts, Cbl-C, BPdc in next 5 sts, Cbl-B, BPdc in next 5 sts, hdc in last st, turn.

Row 21: Ch 2, BPdc in next 2 sts, Cbl-A, BPdc in next 3 sts, Cbl-C, BPdc in next 7 sts, Cbl-B, BPdc in next 4 sts, hdc in last st, turn.

Row 23: Ch 2, BPdc in next 2 sts, Cbl-A, BPdc in next 2 sts, Cbl-C, BPdc in next 9 sts, Cbl-B, BPdc in next 3 sts, hdc in last st, turn. Rep rows 1–23 until panel measures 52 (56, 60, 60, 60)"/132 (142, 152.5, 152.5, 152.5)cm from beg. Fasten off.

Panel C (make 1)

Ch 13 (19, 25, 25, 31).

Foundation row (WS): Dc in 4th ch from hook and in each ch across, turn—11 (17, 23, 23, 29) sts.

Rows 1–2: Ch 2, *BPdc in next 3 sts**, FPdc in next 3 sts; rep from * across, ending last rep at **, hdc in last st, turn.

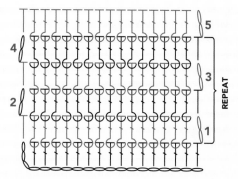

FOUNDATION ROW

Fig. 4: Panel C pattern

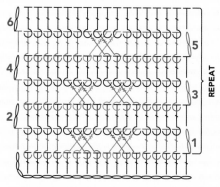

FOUNDATION ROW

Fig. 5: Panel D pattern

Rows 3–4: Ch 2, *FPdc in next 3 sts**, BPdc in next 3 sts; rep from * across, ending last rep at **, hdc in last st, turn.

Rep rows 1–4 until panel measures 22½ (24½, 26½, 26½, 26½)"/57 (62, 67.5, 67.5, 67.5)cm from beg.

Panel D (make 2)

These are the panels for the top of the sleeve. You'll first establish the cabling up the center of the panel in the first few rows. Then, as you increase the number of sts on the sides as indicated, be sure to work the cables in the middle as established.

SPECIAL STITCHES

Cable A (Cbl-A): Sk next 2 sts, FPtr around the post of next 2 sts, BPtr around the post of 1st skipped st, BPtr around the post of 2nd skipped st.

Cable B (Cbl-B): Sk next 2 sts, BPtr around the post of next 2 sts, FPtr around the post of 1st skipped st, FPtr around the post of 2nd skipped st.

Cable C (Cbl-C): Sk next 2 sts, FPtr around the post of next 2 sts, FPtr around the post of 1st skipped st, FPtr around the post of 2nd skipped st.

PATTERN STITCH

Ch 20.

Foundation row: Dc in 4th ch from hook and in each ch across, turn—18 sts.

Row 1 (RS): Ch 2, BPdc in next 4 sts, Cbl-A, Cbl-B, BPdc in next 4 sts, hdc in last st, turn.

Row 2: Ch 2, FPdc around the post of every front raised st; BPdc around the post of every back raised st, hdc in last st, turn.

Row 3: Ch 2, BPdc in next 4 sts, Cbl-B, Cbl-A, BPdc in next 4 sts, hdc in last st, turn.

Row 4: Ch 2, FPdc around the post of every front raised st; BPdc around the post of every back raised st, hdc in last st, turn.

Row 5: Ch 2, BPdc in next 6 sts, Cbl-C, BPdc in next 6 sts, hdc in last st, turn.

Row 6: Ch 2, FPdc around the post of every front raised st; BPdc around the post of every back raised st, hdc in last st, turn.

Rep rows 1–6 for pattern.

Work in pattern stitch, inc 1 st at beg and end of row 2 and every other row 9 times more; then inc 1 st at beg and end of every row until 68 (68, 68, 76, 76) sts are on work; work even until panel measures 18½ (19, 19½, 20, 20)"/47 (48.5, 49.5, 51, 51)cm from beg. Remember as you do the increases to maintain the cabling up the center of the panel.

Panel E-1 (make 1 for L, XL, and XXL only)

SPECIAL STITCHES

BPdc2tog: (Yo, insert hook from back to front to back again around next st, yo, draw yarn through st, yo, draw yarn through 2 loops on hook) twice, yo, draw yarn through 3 loops on hook.

FPdc2tog: (Yo, insert hook from front to back to front again around next st, yo, draw yarn through st, yo, draw yarn through 2 loops on hook) twice, yo, draw yarn through 3 loops on hook.

Cable A (Cbl-A): Sk next st, FPdc around the post of next st, FPdc around the post of last skipped st.

PATTERN STITCH

Ch 10.

Foundation row: Dc in 4th ch from hook and in each ch across, turn—8 sts.

Row 1: Ch 2, BPdc in next 2 sts, Cbl-A, BPdc in next 2 sts, hdc in last st, turn.

Row 2: Ch 2, FPdc in next 2 sts, BPdc in next 2 sts, FPdc in next 2 sts, hdc in last st, turn.

Rows 3–54: Rep rows 1–2.

Row 55: Ch 2, BPdc2tog in next 2 sts, Cbl-A, BPdc in next 2 sts, hdc in last st, turn.

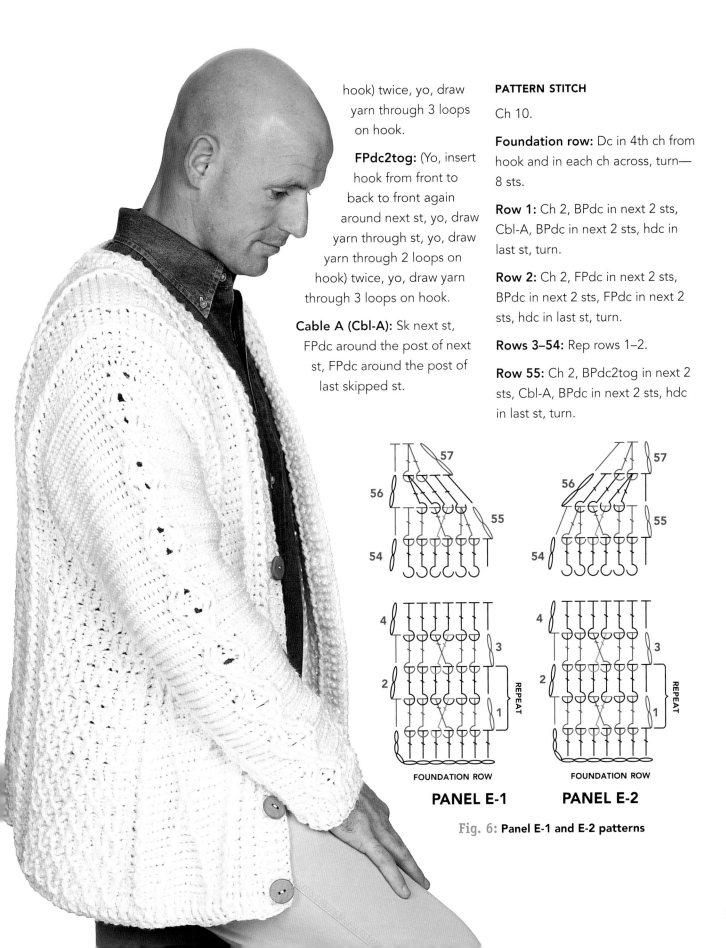

PANEL E-1 **PANEL E-2**

Fig. 6: Panel E-1 and E-2 patterns

Row 56: Ch 2, sk next st, FPdc2tog in next 2 sts, BPdc in next 2 sts, hdc in last st, turn.

Row 57: Ch 2, sk next st, BPdc2tog in next 2 sts, hdc in last st. Fasten off.

Panel E-2 (make 1 for L, XL, and XXL only)

SPECIAL STITCHES

BPdc2tog: (Yo, insert hook from back to front to back again around next st, yo, draw yarn through st, yo, draw yarn through 2 loops on hook) twice, yo, draw yarn through 3 loops on hook.

FPdc2tog: (Yo, insert hook from front to back to front again around next st, yo, draw yarn through st, yo, draw yarn through 2 loops on hook) twice, yo, draw yarn through 3 loops on hook.

PATTERN STITCH

Work same as Panel E-1 through Row 54.

Row 55: Ch 2, BPdc in next 2 sts, Cbl-A, BPdc2tog in next 2 sts, hdc in last st, turn.

Row 56: Ch 2, BPdc in next 2 sts, FPdc2tog in next 2 sts, sk next st, hdc in last st, turn.

Row 57: Ch 2, BPdc2tog in next 2 sts, sk next st, hdc in last st.

Fasten off.

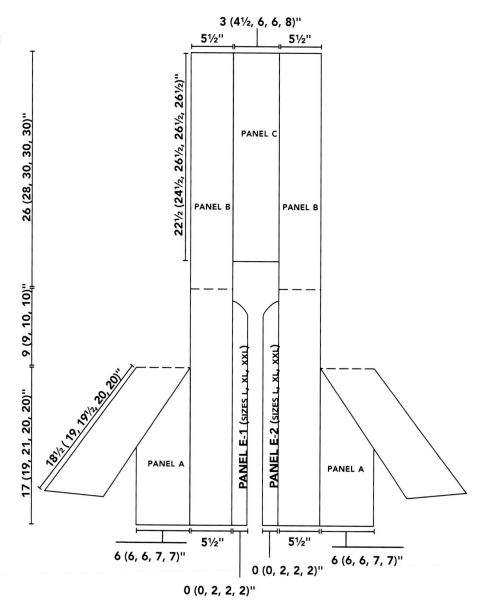

Fig. 7: **Sweater diagram**

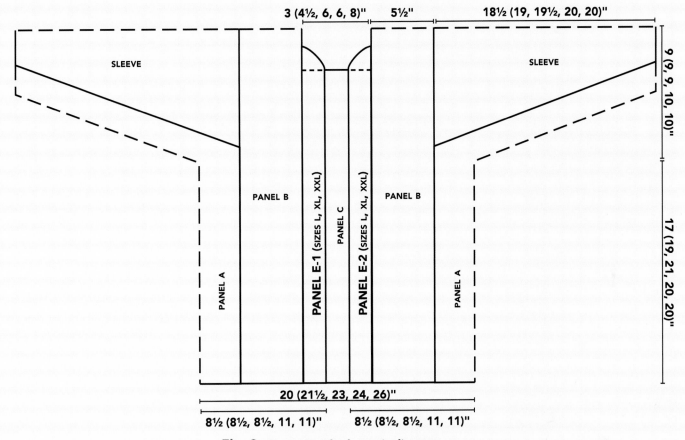

3 (4½, 6, 6, 8)" **5½"** **18½ (19, 19½, 20, 20)"**

SLEEVE

SLEEVE

9 (9, 9, 10, 10)"

PANEL B

PANEL B

PANEL E-1 (SIZES L, XL, XXL)

PANEL C

PANEL E-2 (SIZES L, XL, XXL)

PANEL A

PANEL A

17 (19, 21, 20, 20)"

20 (21½, 23, 24, 26)"

8½ (8½, 8½, 11, 11)" **8½ (8½, 8½, 11, 11)"**

Fig. 8: Constructed schematic diagram

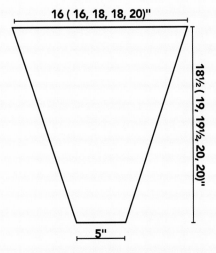

16 (16, 18, 18, 20)"

18½ (19, 19½, 20, 20)"

5"

Fig. 9: Sleeve diagram

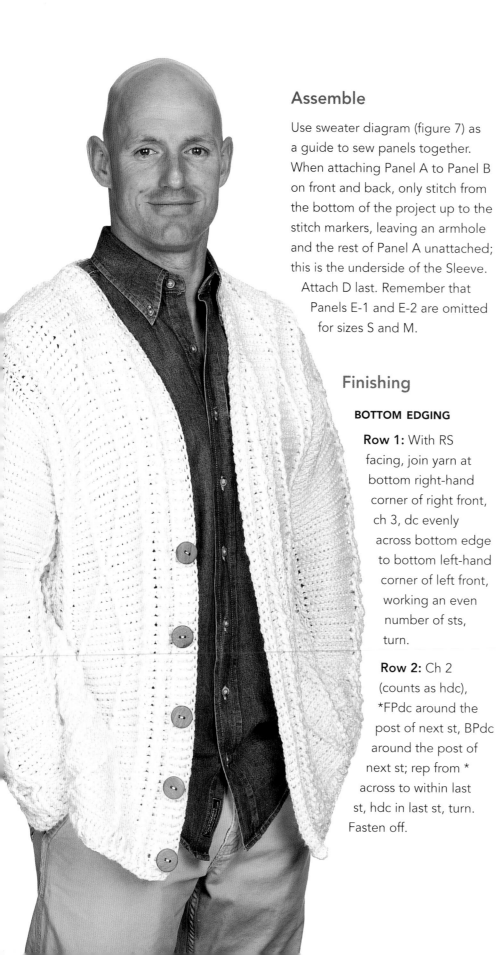

Assemble

Use sweater diagram (figure 7) as a guide to sew panels together. When attaching Panel A to Panel B on front and back, only stitch from the bottom of the project up to the stitch markers, leaving an armhole and the rest of Panel A unattached; this is the underside of the Sleeve. Attach D last. Remember that Panels E-1 and E-2 are omitted for sizes S and M.

Finishing

BOTTOM EDGING

Row 1: With RS facing, join yarn at bottom right-hand corner of right front, ch 3, dc evenly across bottom edge to bottom left-hand corner of left front, working an even number of sts, turn.

Row 2: Ch 2 (counts as hdc), *FPdc around the post of next st, BPdc around the post of next st; rep from * across to within last st, hdc in last st, turn. Fasten off.

SLEEVE EDGING

Rnd 1: With RS facing, join yarn at seam on cuff edge of one sleeve, ch 3, dc evenly around cuff edge, working an even number of sts, sl st in 3rd ch of beg ch-3 to join, turn.

Rnd 2: Ch 2, *FPdc around the post of next st, BPdc around the post of next st; rep from * around to within last st, FPdc in last st, sl st in 2nd ch of beg ch-3 to join.

Fasten off.

PLACKET

Row 1: With RS facing, join yarn at bottom right-hand corner of right front, ch 3, dc evenly across right front edge, across back next edge, and down left front edge to bottom left-hand corner of left front, working an even number of sts, turn.

Row 2: Working in row 2 of 1 x 1 ribbing pattern for 3 sts, ch 1, sk next st, *work in ribbing pattern for 17 sts, ch 1, sk next st; rep from * 2 more times (4 buttonholes made), work in ribbing pattern across. Fasten off.

Weave in ends.

Yarn Used

Moda Dea Fashionista, 50% acrylic/50% Tencel/Lyocell, 3½oz/100g = 183yd/168m per skein

10 (11, 13, 13, 14) skeins, Ivory (#6113)

The Music Sock

I love how this little sock protects my MP3 player without needing to be strapped onto my bicep or hooked on my belt buckle. I just want to get my player from point A to point B safely, and this project does the trick.

Skill Level

Intermediate

Finished Size

6"/15cm in circumference x 5"/12.5cm tall—one size fits most MP3 players

You Will Need

Color A: 36yd/33m of **3** lightweight yarn, in green
Color B: 17yd/16m of **3** lightweight yarn, in blue
Color C: 10yd/9m of **3** lightweight yarn, in cream
Hook: 3.75mm (size F-5 U.S.) (or size to obtain gauge)
Yarn needle

Stitches Used

Back post double crochet (BPdc)
Chain stitch (ch)
Double crochet (dc)
Front post double crochet (FPdc)
Slip stitch (sl st)

Special Stitches

Front post treble crochet (FPtr): Yo (twice), insert hook from front to back to front again around the post of next designated st, yo, draw yarn though st, (yo, draw yarn through 2 loops on hook) 3 times, sk st behind FPtr just made.
Cable A (Cbl-A): Sk next 2 sts, FPtr around the post of next st, BPdc around the post of 2nd skipped st, FPtr around the post of first skipped st.

Gauge

15 sts x 13 rows = 4"/10cm in pattern stitch
Always take time to check your gauge.

Instructions

With Color A, ch 32, and without twisting ch, join with sl st to first ch to form a ring.

Rnd 1 (RS): Ch 3 (counts as dc), dc in each ch around, sl st to top of beg ch-3 to join—32 dc.

Rnd 2: Ch 3 (counts as dc), *Cbl-A in next 3 sts; rep from * around, sl st to top of beg ch-3 to join.

Rnd 3: Ch 3 (counts as dc), *FPdc around the post of next st, BPdc around the post of next st, FPdc around the post of next st; rep from * around, sl st to top of beg ch-3 to join. Fasten off.

Rnd 4: With RS facing, join Color C with a sl st in first st of rnd 3, rep rnd 3. Fasten off.

Rnds 5–6: With RS facing, join Color B with a sl st in first st, rep rnds 2–3. Fasten off.

Rnd 7: With RS facing, join Color C with a sl st in first st, rep rnd 3. Fasten off.

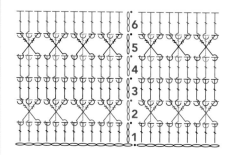

Fig. 1: Stitch pattern

Rnds 8–9: With RS facing, join Color A with a sl st in first st, rep rnds 2–3. Fasten off.

Rnd 10: With RS facing, join Color C with a sl st in first st, rep rnd 3. Fasten off.

Rnds 11–15: Rep rnds 5–9. Do not fasten off after rnd 15.

Rnd 16: Rep rnd 3. Fasten off.

Assemble

Flatten and whipstitch top of rnd 16 to create seam. This is the bottom of the project.

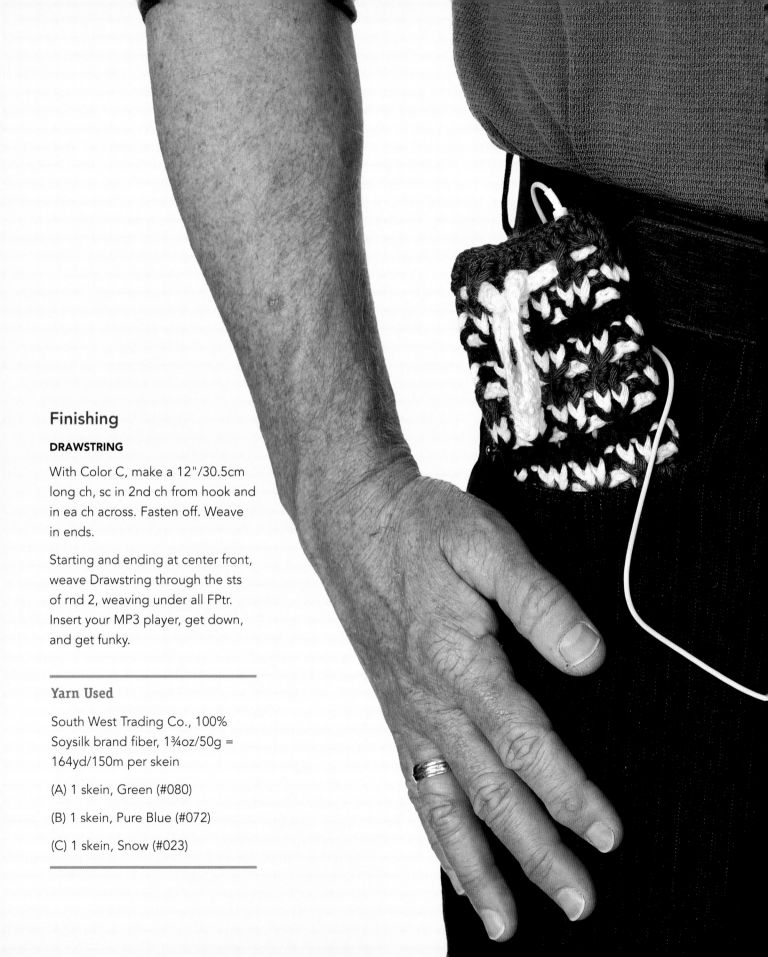

Finishing

DRAWSTRING

With Color C, make a 12"/30.5cm long ch, sc in 2nd ch from hook and in ea ch across. Fasten off. Weave in ends.

Starting and ending at center front, weave Drawstring through the sts of rnd 2, weaving under all FPtr. Insert your MP3 player, get down, and get funky.

Yarn Used

South West Trading Co., 100% Soysilk brand fiber, 1¾oz/50g = 164yd/150m per skein

(A) 1 skein, Green (#080)

(B) 1 skein, Pure Blue (#072)

(C) 1 skein, Snow (#023)

Pure Comfort

Inspired by those familiar French sailor shirts, this roomy boatneck version takes relaxation to a new level, where taking it easy practically becomes a profession. Now there's a job I want.

Instructions

Pattern Stitch

Row 1 (RS): With Color A, ch 1, sc in BL only of each st across, turn.

Rows 2–4: Ch 1, sc in both loops of each st across, turn. Fasten off A, join B.

Row 5: With Color B, ch 1, sc in BL only of each st across, turn, ch 1.

Row 6: Ch 1, sc in both loops of each st across, turn. Fasten off B, join A. Repeat rows 1–6 for pattern stitch.

Back

With Color A, ch 106 (111, 117, 121, 128).

Row 1: Sc in 2nd ch from hook and in ea ch across—105 (110, 116, 120,127) sc.

Starting with row 2, work even in pattern stitch until piece measures 27 (28, 29, 29, 30)"/68.5 (71, 73.5, 73.5, 76)cm from beg. Fasten off.

Front

Work same as Back until piece measures 25 (26, 27, 27, 28)"/63.5 (66, 68.5, 68.5, 71)cm from beg, ending with a WS row.

Skill Level
Experienced

Finished Size
Sizes: S (M, L, XL, XXL): 38 (40, 42, 44, 46)"/96.5 (101.5, 106.5, 112, 117)cm
Sweater shown in size XXL.

You Will Need
Color A: 1582 (1708, 1852, 1870, 2040)yd/1447 (1562, 1694, 1710, 1866)m of **3** lightweight yarn, in white
Color B: 950 (1025, 1111, 1123, 1224)yd/869 (938, 1017, 1028, 1120)m of **3** lightweight yarn, in navy blue
Hook: 3.25mm (size D-3 U.S.) (*or size to obtain gauge*)
Yarn needle
Long sewing pins

Stitches Used
Chain stitch (ch)
Single crochet (sc)
Slip stitch (sl st)

Gauge
22 sts x 24 rows = 4"/10cm in pattern stitch
Always take time to check your gauge.

SHAPE FIRST SHOULDER

Next row: Work in pattern stitch across first 26 (27, 29, 30, 32) sts, turn, leaving rem sts unworked. Cont in pattern stitch until piece measures 27 (28, 29, 29, 30)"/68.5 (71, 73.5, 73.5, 76)cm from beg. Fasten off.

SHAPE SECOND SHOULDER

Next row: Sk 53 (56, 58, 60, 63) sts to the left of last st made in first row of first shoulder, join yarn in next st, work in pattern st across, turn—26 (27, 29, 30, 32) sts. Cont in pattern stitch until piece measures 27 (28, 29, 29, 30)"/68.5 (71, 73.5, 73.5, 76)cm from beg. Fasten off.

Hint: Be sure that you have worked the same total number of rows on the back and front pieces so that the stripes line up when you assemble them.

Sleeve (make 2)

With Color A, ch 73 (75, 78, 81, 83). **Row 1:** Sc into 2nd ch from hook and into each ch across—72 (74, 77, 80, 82) sc.

Work even in pattern stitch for 2 rows.

Continue in pattern stitch, inc 1 st at beg and end of every 5th row until 86 (88, 91, 94, 100) sts are on work. Work even until sleeve measures 8 (9, 10, 11, 12)"/20.5 (23, 25.5, 28, 30.5)cm from beg. Fasten off.

Assemble

Sew shoulder seams. Fold sleeves in half lengthwise, matching fold to shoulder seam, sew tops of sleeves to front and back. Sew sleeve and side seams.

Finishing

BOTTOM TRIM

Rnd 1: With RS facing, join Color B at one side seam on bottom edge, ch 1, sc evenly around, sl st in first sc to join. Fasten off.

NECK TRIM

Starting at shoulder seam, work same as bottom trim around neckline.

SLEEVE TRIM

Starting at underarm seam, work same as bottom trim around sleeve edge. Rep sleeve trim around other sleeve.

Weave in ends.

Yarn Used

Patons Grace, 100% mercerized cotton, 1¾oz/50g = 136yd/125m per skein

(A) 12 (13, 14, 14, 15) skeins, Snow (#60005)

(B) 7 (8, 9, 9, 9) skeins, Marine (#60110)

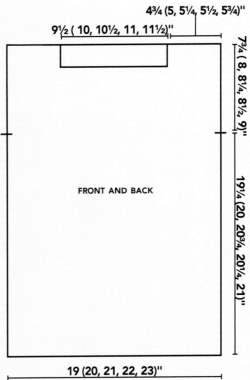

4¾ (5, 5¼, 5½, 5¾)"

9½ (10, 10½, 11, 11½)"

7¾ (8, 8¼, 8½, 9)"

19¼ (20, 20¾, 20¼, 21)"

FRONT AND BACK

19 (20, 21, 22, 23)"

Fig. 1: Front and back diagram

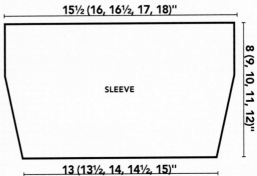

15½ (16, 16½, 17, 18)"

8 (9, 10, 11, 12)"

SLEEVE

13 (13½, 14, 14½, 15)"

Fig. 2: Sleeve diagram

Weekend Turtleneck

Don't worry—this sweater will look great any day of the week. I just gave it this name because bulky weight yarn combined with tall stitches makes for a very quick project. You can start it on Saturday and wear it to work Monday morning.

Instructions

1 x 1 Ribbing Pattern

Ch required number of sts.

Row 1: Dc in 4th ch from hook and in ea ch across, turn.

Row 2: Ch 2 (counts as hdc), *FPdc around the post of next st, BPdc around the post of next st; rep from * across to within last st, hdc in last st, turn.

Rep row 2 for pattern.

PATTERN STITCH

Row 1: Ch 3, dc in each st across, turn.

Rep row 1 for pattern.

Skill Level
Experienced

Finished Size
Sizes: S (M, L, XL, XXL): 39 (42, 44, 46, 48)"/99 (106.5, 112, 117, 122)cm
Sweater shown in size L.

You Will Need
844 (931, 1008, 1080, 1189)yd/772 (852, 922, 988, 1088)m of **5** bulky weight yarn
Hook: 6.50mm (size K-10½ U.S.) (*or size to obtain gauge*)
Yarn needle

Stitches Used
Back post double crochet (BPdc)
Chain stitch (ch)
Double crochet (dc)
Front post double crochet (FPdc)
Half double crochet (hdc)
Single Crochet (sc)
Slip stitch (sl st)

Gauge
11 sts x 6 rows = 4"/10cm in dc
Always take time to check your gauge.

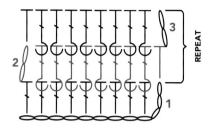

Fig. 1: 1 x 1 ribbing pattern

Back

Ch 56 (60, 62, 66, 68).

Work in 1 x 1 ribbing pattern—54 (58, 60, 64, 66) sts.

Work even in pattern stitch until piece measures 15 (15½, 16, 16, 16½)"/38 (39.5, 40.5, 40.5, 42)cm from beg.

SHAPE ARMHOLE

Next row: Sl st in each of first 8 sts, ch 3, dc in each st across to within last 7 sts, turn, leaving rem sts unworked—40 (44, 46, 50, 52) sts.

Work even in pattern stitch until piece measures 24 (25, 26, 26½, 27½)"/61 (63.5, 66, 67.5, 70)cm from beg.

Last row: Ch 3, dc in each of next 12 (13, 13, 15, 15) sts, hdc in each of next 14 (16, 18, 18, 20) sts, dc in each of last 13 (14, 14, 16, 16) sts. Fasten off.

Front

Work same as for back until front is 1 row less than finished back.

Last row: Ch 3, dc in each of next 12 (13, 13, 15, 15) sts, sc in each of next 14 (16, 18, 18, 20) sts, dc in each of last 13 (14, 14, 16, 16) sts. Fasten off.

Sleeve (make 2)

Ch 24 (26, 28, 28, 30). Work in 1 x 1 ribbing pattern—22 (24, 26, 26, 28) sts.

Work even in pattern stitch for 2 rows; then working in pattern stitch, inc 1 st at end of every row until 50 (52, 54, 58, 60) sts are on work; work even until piece measures 22 (22, 23, 23, 24)"/56 (56, 58.5, 58.5, 61)cm from beg. Fasten off.

Assemble

Sew shoulder seams. Set in sleeves. Sew lower edge of sleeve to armhole shaping. Sew sleeve seams.

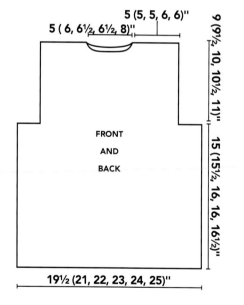

Fig. 2: Front and back diagram

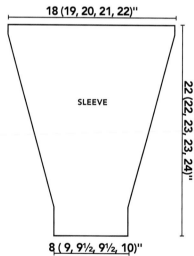

Fig. 3: Sleeve diagram

Finishing

COLLAR

Rnd 1: With RS facing, join yarn at 1 shoulder seam on neck edge, ch 3, dc evenly around neck edge, working an even number of sts, sl st in 3rd ch of beg ch-3 to join.

Rnd 2: Ch 2 (counts as hdc), *FPdc around the post of next st, BPdc around the post of next st; rep from * around to within last st, FPdc around the post of next st, sl st in 2nd ch of beg ch-2 to join.

Rnds 3–5: Rep rnd 2. Fasten off.

Weave in ends.

Yarn Used

Patons Rumor, 84% acrylic/15% alpaca/1% polyester, 2.8oz/80g = 84yd/77m per skein

11 (12, 12, 13, 15) skeins, Duberry Heather (#69530)

Hurry Sundown

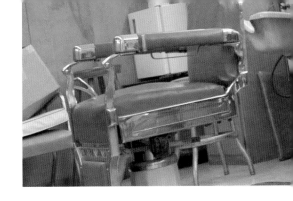

Here's an updated version of a classic cardigan. Alternating green and blue stripes are contrasted with creamy textured cables. Wear the collar up or down—it's your choice—either way you'll be stylin' on a sunset walk or a Saturday morning trip to the barber shop.

Instructions

1 x 1 Ribbing Pattern

Ch required number of sts.

Foundation row (WS): Dc in 4th ch from hook and in ea ch across, turn.

Row 1: Ch 2 (counts as hdc), *FPdc around the post of next st, BPdc around the post of next st; rep from * across to within last 2 sts, FPdc around the post of next st, hdc in last st, turn.

Row 2: Ch 2 (counts as hdc), *BPdc around the post of next st, FPdc around the post of next st; rep from * across to within last 2 sts, BPdc around the post of next st, hdc in last st, turn.

PATTERN STITCH

Fasten off A, join Color B.

Rows 1–2: With Color B, ch 1, sc in ea st across, turn. Fasten off B, join Color A.

Skill Level
Experienced

Finished Size
Sizes: S (M, L, XL, XXL): 40 (43, 44½, 47, 48½)"/101.5 (109, 113, 119.5, 123)cm without lapels; 41½ (44½, 46, 48½, 50)"/105.5 (113, 117, 123, 127)cm with lapels overlapped.
Sweater shown in size L.

You Will Need
Color A: 1231 (1364, 1540, 1604, 1793)yd/1126 (1247, 1408, 1467, 1640)m of (**5**) bulky weight yarn, in cream
Color B: 336 (380, 420, 437, 489)yd/308 (348, 384, 400, 447)m of (**5**) bulky weight yarn, in blue
Color C: 336 (380, 420, 437, 489)yd/308 (348, 384, 400, 447)m of (**5**) bulky weight yarn, in green
Hook: 5.50mm (size I-9 U.S.) (*or size to obtain gauge*)
Yarn needle
Long sewing pins

Stitches Used
Back post double crochet (BPdc)
Chain stitch (ch)
Double crochet (dc)
Front post double crochet (FPdc)
Half double crochet (hdc)
Slip stitch (sl st)

Special Stitches

Front post double treble crochet (FPdtr): Yo (3 times), insert hook from front to back to front again around the post of designated st, yo, draw yarn through st, (yo, draw yarn through 2 lps on hk) 4 times.

Double crochet two together (dc2tog): (Yo, insert hook in next st, yo, draw yarn through st, yo, draw yarn through 2 lps on hk) twice, yo, draw yarn through 3 lps on hook.

Gauge

12 sts x 10 rows = 4"/10cm in pattern stitch

Always take time to check your gauge.

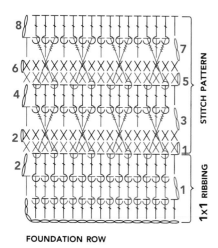

FOUNDATION ROW

Fig. 1: Pattern stitch

Row 3 (RS): With Color A, ch 2, *sk next 2 sts, FPdtr around the post of next corresponding post st 3 rows below, dc in 2nd skipped st, FPdtr around the post of post st 3 rows below 1st skipped st, sk st behind FPdtr just made, dc in next st in current row; rep from * across, ending with hdc in last st, turn.

Row 4: Ch 2 (counts as hdc), *BPdc around the post of next st, FPdc around the post of next st; rep from * across to within last 2 sts, BPdc around the post of next st, hdc in last st, turn. Fasten off A, join Color C.

Rows 5–6: With Color C, ch 1, sc in ea st across, turn. Fasten off C, join Color A.

Rows 7–8: Rep rows 3–4.

Rep rows 1–8 for pattern stitch.

Body

Note: Body of sweater is crocheted in one piece.

Ch 123 (131, 135, 143, 147).

Work 1 x 1 ribbing pattern through row 2—121, 129, 133, 141, 145 sts.

Begin pattern stitch and work even in pattern stitch until piece measures 16 (18, 20, 20, 22)"/40.5 (45.5, 51, 51, 56)cm from the beginning, ending with a RS row.

LEFT FRONT

Work in pattern stitch across first 21 (23, 24, 26, 27) sts, turn, leaving rem sts unworked—21 (23, 24, 26, 27) sts. Work even in pattern stitch until piece measures 22 (24, 26, 26, 28)"/56 (61, 66, 66, 71)cm from beg, ending with a WS row.

SHAPE NECKLINE

Working in established pattern, dec 1 st at end of every RS row 4 times, then work even in pattern until piece measures 26 (28, 30, 30, 32)"/66 (71, 76, 76, 81.5)cm from beg. Fasten off.

BACK

Return to last row of Body, sk 15 sts to the left of last st made in first row of left front, join next color in sequence in next st, starting in same st, work in even pattern stitch across next 49 (53, 55, 59, 61) sts, turn, leaving rem sts unworked. Work even in pattern until piece measures 26 (28, 30, 30, 32)"/66 (71, 76, 76, 81.5)cm from beg. Fasten off.

RIGHT FRONT

Return to last row of Body, sk 15 sts to the left of last st made in first row of back, join next color in sequence in next st, starting in same st, work in even pattern stitch across—21 (23, 24, 26, 27) sts. Work even in pattern stitch until piece measures 22 (24, 26, 26, 28)"/56 (61, 66, 66, 71)cm from beg, ending with a WS row.

SHAPE NECKLINE

Working in established pattern, dec 1 st at end of every WS row 4 times, then work even in pattern until piece measures 26 (28, 30, 30, 32)"/66 (71, 76, 76, 81.5)cm from beg. Fasten off.

Sleeve (make 2)

Ch 27 (27, 27, 31, 31).

Work 1 x 1 ribbing pattern through row 2—25 (25, 25, 29, 29) sts.

Work even in pattern stitch for 8 rows. Working in pattern stitch, inc 1 st at end of every row until 48 (48, 54, 54, 60) sts are on work, then work even until sleeve measures 18½ (19, 19½, 20, 20½)"/47 (48.5, 49.5, 51, 52)cm from beg. Be sure to incorporate cables as enough sts are added.

SHAPE SLEEVE CAP

Working in established pattern stitch, dec 1 st at beg of every row 7 (7, 1, 1, 0) times, then dec 1 st at beg and end of every row 18 (18, 24, 24, 30) times. Fasten off.

Assemble

Sew shoulder seams. Set in sleeves. Sew sleeve and side seams.

Finishing

COLLAR

Foundation row: With WS facing, join yarn in top left-hand corner of left front, ch 1, dc evenly across neck edge to top right-hand corner of right front, turn. Work rows 1–2 of 1 x 1 ribbing pattern. Fasten off.

RIGHT LAPEL

Foundation row: With WS facing, join yarn in top right-hand corner of right front at base of collar, ch 1, dc evenly across right front edge to bottom edge, turn. Work rows 1–2 of 1 x 1 ribbing pattern. Fasten off.

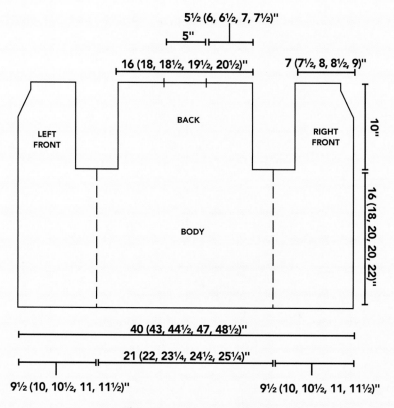

Fig. 2: **Sweater diagram**

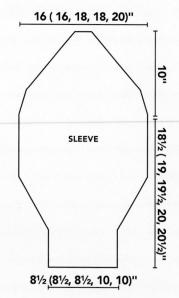

Fig. 3: **Sleeve diagram**

LEFT LAPEL

Foundation row: With WS facing, join yarn in bottom left-hand corner of left front, ch 1, dc evenly across left front edge to base of collar, turn. Work rows 1–2 of 1 x 1 ribbing pattern. Fasten off.

Weave in ends.

Yarn Used

Red Heart Casual Cot'n, 61% acrylic/29% cotton/10% polyester, 4oz/113g = 140yd/128m per skein

(A) 9 (10, 11, 12, 13) skeins, Creamy (#3217)

(B) 3 (3, 3, 4, 4) skeins, Majestic (#3339)

(C) 3 (3, 3, 4, 4) skeins, Ivy (#3362)

Metrocabled

Stash this cabled sweater at work, and it can take you from the office to a hot date. If that certain someone wants to meet for cocktails, you know it'll make you look fantastic.

Instructions

Note: *Torso and sleeves are worked in the round separately, then joined and worked as one piece from the underarm to the neck.*

Cable Pattern

Ch required number of sts, and without twisting ch, join with a sl st to form ring.

Rnd 1: Ch 3 (counts as dc), dc in each ch around, sl st in top of beg ch-3 to join.

Rnds 2–3: Ch 2, BPdc in next st, *FPdc in next 3 sts**, BPdc in next 2 sts; rep from * around, ending last rep at **, sl st in top of beg ch-2 to join.

Rnd 4: Ch 2, BPdc in next 6 sts, *sk next st, FPdc in next 2 sts, FPdc in last skipped st**, BPdc in next 7 sts; rep from * around, ending last rep at **, sl st in top of beg ch-2.

Rnd 5: Ch 2, BPdc in next 6 sts, *FPdc in next 3 sts**, BPdc in next 7 sts; rep from * around, ending last rep at **, sl st in top of beg ch-2.

Rep rnds 4–5 for cable pattern.

Skill Level
Experienced

Finished Size
Sizes: S (M, L, XL, XXL): 36 (40, 44, 47, 51)"/91.5 (101.5, 112, 119.5, 129.5)cm
Sweater shown in size L.

You Will Need
1512 (1764, 1932, 2184, 2352)yd/1383 (1614, 1768, 1998, 2152)m of (**5**) bulky weight yarn
Hook: 6.00mm (size J-10 U.S.) (*or size to obtain gauge*)
Yarn needle
Long sewing pins
Stitch marker

Stitches Used
Back post double crochet (BPdc)
Chain stitch (ch)
Double crochet (dc)
Front post double crochet (FPdc)
Slip stitch (sl st)

Special Stitches
Back post double crochet 3 together (BPdc3tog): (Yo, insert hook from front to back to front again around the post of designated st, yo, draw yarn through st, yo, draw yarn through 2 lps on hook) 3 times, yo, draw yarn through 4 lps on hook.

Gauge
11 sts x 10 rows = 4"/10cm in cable pattern
Always take time to check your gauge.

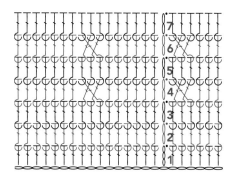

Fig. 1: Cable pattern

Torso

Ch 100 (110, 120, 130, 140), and without twisting ch, join with a sl st to form ring. Work in cable pattern until piece measures 17½"/44.5cm from beg, ending with a rnd 5 of pattern. Fasten off.

Sleeve (make 2)

Ch 30, and without twisting ch, join with a sl st to form ring. Work in cable pattern until piece measures 3"/7.5cm from beg. Cont in cable pattern, inc 1 st at beg of each rnd, maintaining cable pattern as established, until you have 44 (47, 50, 52, 55) sts per rnd.

Note: you will have enough sts to start adding another cable after each 7 increases.

Work even in cable pattern until sleeve measures 14½ (15½, 16, 16½, 17)"/37 (39.5, 40.5, 42, 43)cm from beg or desired length to underarm, ending with a rnd 5 of pattern. Fasten off.

Assemble

Flatten torso with beg of rnds on one side. Lay sleeves parallel to torso so that the beg of rnds are facing underarm. Pin where the top of the torso and sleeves meet. The rem rnds of the sweater will be worked all in one piece around, joining the sleeves to the torso.

Bodice

Rnd 1: Join yarn with a FPdc around the post of any st on the top edge of back, *FPdc in each st across to within 1 st of where the sleeve is pinned to the torso, BPdc in next st, FPdc in each st around sleeve to within 1 st of where the sleeve is pinned to the torso, BPdc in next st; rep from * around, FPdc in ea st across to beg of rnd—188 (204, 220, 234, 250) sts, do not join. Work in a spiral. Place marker at beg of rnd and move marker up as work progresses.

Rnd 2: *FPdc in each st across to within 1 st of BPdc, BPdc3tog across next 3 sts; rep from * around, FPdc in ea st across to beg of rnd.

Rnds 3–18 (20, 21, 22, 23): Rep rnd 2—52 (52, 60, 66, 74) sts at end of last rnd. Do not fasten off.

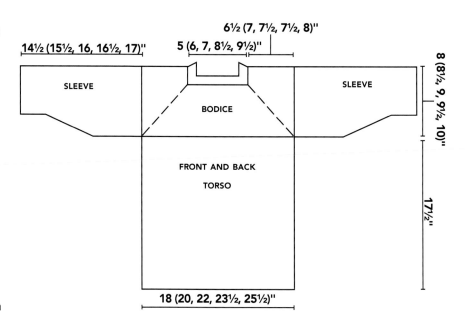

Fig. 2: Assembly diagram

Finishing

NECK RIBBING

Rnd 1: *BPdc in next st, FPdc in next st; rep from * around, do not join—42 (50, 56, 60, 66) sts. Work in a spiral as before.

Rnd 2: Rep rnd 1. At end of rnd 2, sl st in next st to join. Fasten off.

Weave in ends.

Yarn Used

Patons Rumor, 84% acrylic/15% alpaca/1% polyester, 2.8oz/80g = 84yd/77m per skein

18 (21, 23, 26, 28) skeins, Spanish Heather (#69040)

Jock Block Hat & Scarf

It's a challenge for a dude to wear clothes from high school or college without looking foolish. This hat and scarf project will bring back fond memories of when clothes declared that you should just "Relax" and "Choose Life!" At least it did for me.

Instructions

Scarf Pattern Stitch

Row 1: Ch 3 (counts as dc), dc in each dc across, turn.

Row 2: Ch 3 (counts as dc), dc in FL only of ea st across, turn.

Hat

CROWN

With B, ch 75, and without twisting ch, sl st in first ch to form a ring.

Rnd 1: Sc in each ch around, do not join—75 sc. Work in a spiral. Place marker at beg of rnd and move marker up as work progresses.

Rnd 2: *Sc in next 13 sc, sc2tog in next 2 sts; rep from * around—70 sts.

Rnd 3: *Sc in next 12 sc, sc2tog in next 2 sts; rep from * around—65 sts.

Rnd 4: *Sc in next 11 sc, sc2tog in next 2 sts; rep from * around—60 sts.

Cont to dec 2 sts ea rnd as established until 5 sts remain. Fasten off, leaving a long sewing length. Use tail to weave through tops of last 5 sts. Gather and secure.

Skill Level
Beginner

Finished Size
Hat: 24"/61cm in circumference—one
   size fits most adult heads
Scarf: 70"/178cm long—one size fits all

You Will Need
Color A: 124yd/114m of (**5**) bulky
   weight yarn, in brown
Color B: 124yd/114m of (**5**) bulky
   weight yarn, in beige
Color C: 124yd/114m of (**5**) bulky
   weight yarn, in green
Hook: 5.00mm (size H-8 U.S.) (*or size to
   obtain gauge*)
Stitch marker
Yarn needle

Stitches Used
Back post double crochet (BPdc)
Chain stitch (ch)
Double crochet (dc)
Front post double crochet (FPdc)
Half double crochet (hdc)
Single crochet (sc)
Slip stitch (sl st)

Special Stitch
Single crochet two together (sc2tog):
   (Insert hook in next st, yo, draw yarn
   through st) twice, yo, draw yarn
   through 3 lps on hook.

Gauge
12 sts x 13 rows = 4"/10cm in sc; 5
   rows = 4"/10cm in dc
Always take time to check your gauge.

TRIM

Rnd 1: With RS facing, working across opposite side of foundation ch, join Color B with sl st to any st along foundation ch, ch 1, 2 sc in first sc, sc in ea around, sl st to first sc to join—76 sc. Fasten off.

FIRST RIBBING HALF

Row 1: With RS facing, join Color A with sl st in any sc in rnd 1, ch 3 (counts as dc), dc in next 37 sts, turn—38 dc.

Row 2: Ch 2, *FPdc around the post of next dc, BPdc around the post of next dc; rep from * across, ending with hdc in last st, turn—38 sts.

Rows 2-5: Rep row 1. Fasten off.

SECOND RIBBING HALF

Row 1: With RS facing, join C with sl st in 1st st to the left of last st made in row 1 of First Ribbing Half, ch 3 (counts as dc), dc in next 37 sts, turn—38 dc.

Row 2: Rep row 2 of First Ribbing Half. Fasten off.

Seam ribbing where Ribbing Halves meet.

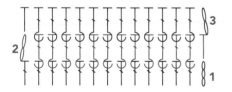

CROWN

BOTTOM EDGING

Fig. 1: Hat ribbing and edging pattern

Scarf

FIRST HALF

With A, ch 13.

Row 1 (RS): Dc in 4th ch from hook and in each ch across, turn—11 dc.

Row 2: Ch 3 (counts as dc), dc in FL only of ea st across, turn—11 dc.

Fasten off A, join B.

Starting with row 1 of scarf pattern stitch, work in the following color sequence: *2 rows C; 2 rows B; 2 rows A; rep from * three times; then work 2 rows C; 24 rows B. Fasten off.

SECOND HALF

With RS facing, working across opposite side of foundation ch, join B in first ch. Starting with Row 1 of scarf pattern stitch, work in the following color sequence: 24 rows B; *2 rows A; 2 rows C; rep from * twice. Fasten off.

EDGING

Rnd 1: With RS facing, join A with sc to any corner of scarf, work 2 more sc in same corner, sc evenly around, working 3 sc in ea corner and 2 sc in the end of each row, sl st to first sc to join.

SIDE PANEL

Row 1: With scarf lengthwise and RS facing, join A to center st of top right-hand corner of scarf, ch 3 (counts as dc), dc in each st across long side of scarf, do not turn. Fasten off.

Row 2: With RS facing, join C in first st of last row, ch 3 (counts as dc), dc in ea dc across. Fasten off.

Weave in ends.

Yarn Used

Moda Dea Metro, 94% acrylic/6% nylon, 3½oz/100g = 124yd/114m per skein

(A) 1 skein, Chocolate (#9340)

(B) 1 skein, Wheat (#9321)

(C) 1 skein, Wasabi (#9632)

SIDE PANEL

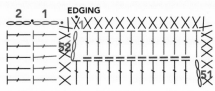

SCARF FIRST HALF

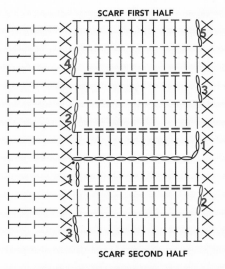

SCARF SECOND HALF

Fig. 2: Scarf pattern

For the Prepsters

I so wanted to be preppy in school, but my sister bleached my hair and gave me a Mohawk. For some reason, I got a reputation as a punk. This sweater brings out my inner preppy and helps me forget the Mohawk.

Instructions

Cabled Ribbing Pattern

Ch indicated number.

Row 1 (RS): Dc in 4th ch from hook and in each ch across, turn.

Row 2: Ch 2 (counts as hdc), *BPdc in next 2 sts, FPdc in next 2 sts; rep from * across, ending with a hdc in last st, turn.

Row 3: Ch 2 (counts as hdc), *sk next st, FPdc in next st, FPdc in last skipped st, BPdc in next 2 sts; rep from * across, ending with a hdc in last st, turn.

Row 4: Ch 2 (counts as hdc), *BPdc in next 2 sts, FPdc in next 2 sts; rep from * across, ending with a hdc in last st, turn.

Rows 5–6: Repeat rows 3–4.

PATTERN STITCH

Row 1: Ch 1, sc in first st, *dc in next st, sc in next st; rep from * across, turn.

Row 2: Ch 1, sc in first dc, *dc in next sc, sc in next dc; rep from * across, turn.

Rep row 2 for pattern stitch.

Skill Level
Experienced

Finished Size
Sizes: S (M, L, XL, XXL): 38 (40, 43, 45, 47)"/96.5 (101.5, 109, 114.5, 119.5)cm
Sweater shown in size M.

You Will Need
Color A: 1515 (1660, 1813, 1943, 2168)yd/1387 (1520, 1660, 1779, 1985)m of **(4)** medium weight yarn, in teal
Color B: 151 (166, 181, 194, 217)yd/139 (152, 166, 179, 199)m of **(4)** medium weight yarn, in cream
Color C: 151 (166, 181, 194, 217)yd/139 (152, 166, 179, 199)m of **(4)** medium weight yarn, in brown
Hook: 5.00mm (size H-8 U.S.) (*or size to obtain gauge*)
Stitch marker
Yarn needle

Stitches Used
Back post double crochet (BPdc)
Chain stitch (ch)
Double crochet (dc)
Front post double crochet (FPdc)
Single crochet (sc)
Slip stitch (sl st)

Special Stitches

Single crochet two together (sc2tog): (Insert hook in next st, yo, draw yarn through st) twice, yo, draw yarn through 3 lps on hook.

Front post double crochet 3 together (FPdc3tog): (Yo, insert hook from back to front to back again around the post of designated st, yo, draw yarn through st, yo, draw yarn through 2 lps on hook) 3 times, yo, draw yarn through 4 lps on hook.

Note: Entire sweater is made in pattern stitch unless otherwise indicated.

Gauge

15 sts x 13 rows = 4"/10cm in pattern stitch
Always take time to check your gauge.

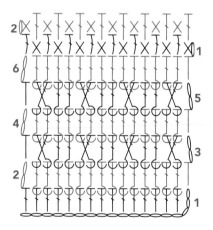

Fig. 1: Cabled ribbing pattern

Back

With Color A, ch 74 (78, 82, 86, 90).

Work in cabled ribbing pattern—72 (76, 80, 84, 88) sts.

With Color A, work in pattern stitch until piece measures 10½"/26.5cm from beg.

Fasten off A, join Color B.

Work in pattern stitch in the following color sequence: 2 rows B; 2 rows A; 4 rows C; 2 rows A; 2 rows B. Fasten off B, join Color A.

With Color A, work in pattern stitch until piece measures 15 (15½, 16, 16, 16½)"/38 (39.5, 40.5, 40.5, 42)cm from beg.

SHAPE ARMHOLE

Next row: Work in pattern stitch across to within last 10 sts, turn, leaving rem sts unworked—62 (66, 70, 74, 78) sts.

Next row: Work in pattern stitch across to within last 10 sts, turn, leaving rem sts unworked—52 (56, 60, 64, 68) sts.

Work even in pattern stitch until piece measures 23 (24, 25, 25½, 26½)"/58.5 (61, 63.5, 65, 67.5)cm from beg, ending with a WS row.

SHAPE FIRST SHOULDER

Next row: Work in pattern stitch across first 12 (14, 16, 18, 20) sts, turn, leaving rem sts unworked—12 (14, 16, 18, 20) sts.

Work even in pattern stitch until piece measures 24 (25, 26, 26½, 27½)"/61 (63.5, 66, 67.5, 70)cm from beg. Fasten off.

SHAPE SECOND SHOULDER

Next row: Sk 28 sts to the left of last st made in first row of first shoulder, join yarn in next st, work in pattern stitch across—12 (14, 16, 18, 20) sts.

Work even in pattern stitch until piece measures 24 (25, 26, 26½, 27½)"/61 (63.5, 66, 67.5, 70)cm from beg. Fasten off.

Front

Work same as back through 2 rows of armhole shaping. Place stitch marker in center st of current row, begin working armhole shaping as for back, and at the same time begin working V-neck shaping.

SHAPE FIRST SIDE

Work in pattern stitch across to within 2 sts of marker, sc2tog in next 2 sts (dec made), turn—25 (27, 29, 32, 33) sts. Maintaining pattern, dec 1 st at neck edge every other row 12 (12, 13, 14, 15) times. Then dec 1 st at neck edge every row 0 (2, 2, 2, 1) times. Work even in pattern stitch until piece measures 24 (25, 26, 26½, 27½)"/61 (63.5, 66, 67.5, 70)cm from beg. Fasten off.

SHAPE SECOND SIDE

Join yarn in first st to the left of marker, ch 1, sc2tog in first 2 sts, work in pattern stitch across, turn—25 (27, 29, 32, 33) sts. Work same as first side, reversing shaping.

Sleeve (make 2)

With Color A, ch 36 (42, 42, 44, 44). Work in cabled ribbing pattern—34 (40, 40, 42, 42) sts.

Work even in pattern stitch for 4 rows. Fasten off A, join Color B.

Work in pattern stitch in the following color sequence: 2 rows B; 2 rows A; 4 rows C; 2 rows A; 2 rows B; then work in Color A, inc 2 sts at ea end of every 4th row until 56 (60, 64, 68, 76) sts are on work. Work even in pattern stitch until piece measures 18½ (19, 19½, 20, 20½)"/47 (48.5, 49.5, 51, 52)cm from beg.

SHAPE SLEEVE CAP

Dec 1 st at end of next 10 (6, 8, 6, 3) rows. Then, dec 1 st at beg and end of next 20 (24, 25, 28, 33) rows. Fasten off.

Assemble

Sew shoulder seams. Set in sleeves. Sew sleeve and side seams.

Finishing

NECK EDGING

Rnd 1: With WS facing, join yarn along back of neckline, ch 3 (counts as dc), dc evenly around neck opening, being sure that you work one dc at the point of the V, and being sure that you end with an even number of stitches, sl st in top of beg ch-3, turn.

Rnd 2 (RS): Ch 2, *FPdc in next st, BPdc in next st; rep from * around to within one st of dc in the point of the V, FPdc3tog in next 3 sts, rep from * to * around, sl st in top of beg ch-3. Fasten off.

Weave in ends.

Yarn Used

Moda Dea Washable Wool, 100% superwash wool, 3½oz/100g = 166yd/152m per skein

(A) 10 (10, 11, 12, 14) skeins, Teal (#4418)

(B) 1 (1, 2, 2, 2) skeins, Ivory (#4413)

(C) 1 (1, 2, 2 ,2) skeins, Coffee (#4465)

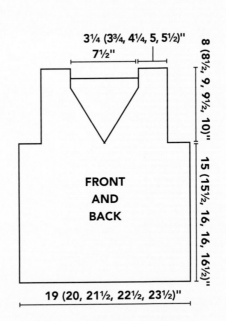

3¼ (3¾, 4¼, 5, 5½)"
7½"
8 (8½, 9, 9½, 10)"
15 (15½, 16, 16, 16½)"
19 (20, 21½, 22½, 23½)"

FRONT AND BACK

Fig. 2: Front and back diagram

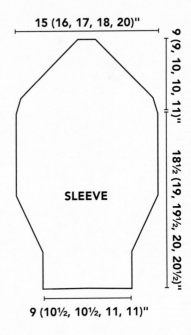

15 (16, 17, 18, 20)"
9 (9, 10, 10, 11)"
18½ (19, 19½, 20, 20½)"
9 (10½, 10½, 11, 11)"

SLEEVE

Fig. 3: Sleeve diagram

Zip It Cabled Vest

Zip up this vest and keep warm without feeling encumbered. The all-over cabling creates a thick, insulating fabric. This project gives you a great introduction to cables, wearables, and adding a zipper.

Instructions

Note: *Work the entire project as one piece, then seam along the shoulders.*

Pattern Stitch

Row 1 (WS): Ch 2, *BPdc around the post of next st, FPdc around the post of next st, BPdc around the post of next st**, FPdc around the posts of next 4 sts; rep from * across, ending last rep at **, hdc in last st, turn.

Row 2: Ch 2, *FPdc around the post of next st, BPdc around the post of next st, FPdc around the post of next st**, BPdc around the posts of next 4 sts; rep from * across, ending last rep at **, hdc in last st, turn.

Row 3: Ch 2, FPdc around the post of every front raised st; BPdc around the post of every back raised st, hdc in last st, turn. (Repeat this for all odd rows.)

Row 4: Ch 2, *sk next 2 sts, FPdc around the post of next st, BPdc around 2nd skipped st, FPdc around 1st skipped st**, BPdc around the posts of next 4 sts; rep from * across, ending last rep at **, hdc in last st, turn.

Row 6: Rep row 4.

Skill Level
Experienced

Finished Size
Sizes: S (M, L, XL, XXL): 40 (42, 44, 46, 49)"/101.5 (106.5, 112, 117, 124.5)cm
Sweater shown in size L.

You Will Need
1650 (1800, 1950, 2100, 2400)yd/1510 (1647, 1784, 1922, 2196)m of (4) medium weight yarn
Hook: 5.00mm (size H-8 U.S.) (*or size to obtain gauge*)
Yarn needle
26"/66cm separating zipper
Coordinating sewing thread
Sewing needle

Stitches Used
Back post double crochet (BPdc)
Chain stitch (ch)
Double crochet (dc)
Front post double crochet (FPdc)
Half double crochet (hdc)
Single crochet (sc)
Slip stitch (sl st)

Gauge
17 sts x 11 rows = 4"/10cm in pattern stitch
Always take time to check your gauge.

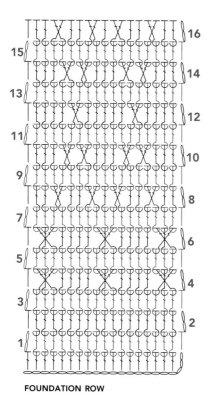

Fig. 1: Pattern stitch

Row 8: Ch 2, FPdc around the post of next st, BPdc around the post of next st, *sk next st, BPdc around the post of next st, FPdc around the post of last skipped st, BPdc around the post of next 2 sts, sk next st, FPdc around the post of next st, BPdc around the post of last skipped st, BPdc around the post of next st; rep from * across to within last 2 sts, FPdc around the post of next st, hdc in last st, turn.

Row 10: Ch 2, FPdc around the post of next st, BPdc around the post of next 2 sts, *sk next st, BPdc around the post of next st, FPdc around the post of last skipped st, sk next st, FPdc around the post of next st, skip next st, BPdc around the post of last skipped st, BPdc around the post of next 3 sts; rep from * across, omitting last BPdc, FPdc around the post of next st, hdc in last st, turn.

Row 12: Ch 2, FPdc around the post of next st, BPdc around the post of next 3 sts, *sk next st, FPdc around the post of next st, FPdc around the post of last skipped st, BPdc around the post of next 5 sts; rep from * across, omitting last 3 BPdc, FPdc around the post of next st, hdc in last st, turn.

Row 14: Ch 2, FPdc around the post of next st, BPdc around the post of next 2 sts, *sk next st, FPdc around the post of next st, BPdc around the post of last skipped st, sk next st, BPdc around the post of next st, FPdc around the post of last skipped st, BPdc around the post of next 3 sts; rep from * across, omitting last BPdc, FPdc around the post of next st, hdc in last st, turn.

Row 16: Ch 2, FPdc around the post of next st, BPdc around the post of next st, *sk next st, FPdc around the post of next st, BPdc around the post of last skipped st, BPdc around the post of next 2 sts, sk next st, BPdc around the post of next st, FPdc around the post of last skipped st, BPdc around the post of next st; rep from * across to within last 2 sts, FPdc around the post of next st, hdc in last st, turn.

Repeat rows 3–16 for pattern stitch.

Body

Ch 175 (182, 189, 196, 210).

Foundation row (RS): Dc into 4th ch from hook and into each st across, turn—173 (180, 187, 194, 208) sts.

Work in pattern st until project measures 15, (15½, 16, 16, 16½)"/38 (39.5, 40.5, 40.5, 42)cm from beg, ending with a WS row.

RIGHT FRONT

Next row: Maintaining pattern as established, work across first 34 (36, 38, 41, 43) sts, turn, leaving rem sts unworked. Work even in pattern stitch as established until project measures 24 (25, 26, 26½, 27½)"/61 (63.5, 66, 67.5, 70)cm from beg, ending with a WS row. Fasten off.

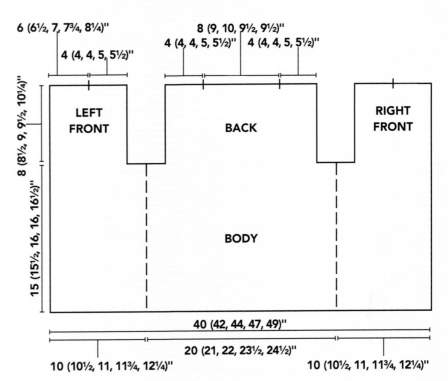

Fig. 2: Vest diagram

BACK

Next row: With RS facing, sk 17 sts to the left of last st made in 1st row of right front, join yarn in next st, starting in same st, work in pattern stitch across next 71 (74, 77, 85, 88) sts, turn, leaving rem sts unworked. Return to last row of Body and skip 4"/10cm, attach and work in pattern as established for 16 (17, 18, 19, 20½)"/40.5 (43, 45.5, 48.5, 52)cm, turn. Work even in pattern stitch as established until project measures 24 (25, 26, 26½, 27½)"/61 (63.5, 66, 67.5, 70)cm from beg, ending with a WS row. Fasten off.

LEFT FRONT

Next row: With RS facing, sk 17 sts to the left of last st made in 1st row of right front, join yarn in next st, starting in same st, work in pattern stitch across next 34 (36, 38, 41, 43) sts, turn, leaving rem sts unworked. Work even in pattern stitch as established until project measures 24 (25, 26, 26½, 27½)"/61 (63.5, 66, 67.5, 70)cm from beg, ending with a WS row. Fasten off.

Assemble

Sew fronts to back across 1st 4 (4, 4, 5, 5½)"/10 (10, 10, 12.5, 14)cm from armhole edge for shoulder seams.

Finishing

ARMHOLE TRIM

Rnd 1: With RS facing, join yarn at center bottom of 1 armhole, ch 1, sc evenly around armhole, sl st in first sc to join. Fasten off.

Rep armhole trim around other armhole.

COLLAR

Row 1: With RS facing, join yarn at top right-hand corner of right front on neck edge, ch 1, sc evenly across neck edge to top left-hand corner of left front, working an odd number of sts, turn.

Row 2: Ch 3 (counts as dc), dc in each sc across, turn.

Row 3: Ch 2, *FPdc around the post of next st, BPdc around the post of next st; rep from * across to within last 2 sts, FPdc around the post of next st, hdc in last st, turn.

Row 4: Ch 2, *BPdc around the post of next st, FPdc around the post of next st; rep from * across to within last 2 sts, BPdc around the post of next st, hdc in last st, turn.

Rows 5–6: Repeat rows 3–4.

Row 7: Rep row 3. Fasten off.

LEFT ZIPPER BAND

Row 1: With WS facing, join yarn at bottom left-hand corner of left front edge, ch 1, sc evenly across left front edge to top edge of collar, turn.

Row 2: Ch 1, sc in BL only of ea sc across. Fasten off.

RIGHT ZIPPER BAND

Row 1: With WS facing, join yarn at top right-hand corner of right front edge at top edge of collar, ch 1, sc evenly across right front edge, turn.

Row 2: Ch 1, sc in BL only of ea sc across. Fasten off.

With sewing thread and sewing needle, sew in zipper on zipper band following manufacturer's instructions.

FACING

Row 1: With RS facing, join yarn in rem lp of first st in row 1 of Right Zipper Band, ch 1, hdc in rem lp of each sc across. Fasten off. Rep facing on row 1 of Left Zipper Band.

Weave in all ends.

Yarn Used

Caron Simply Soft Tweed, 96% acrylic/4% rayon, 3oz/85g = 150yd/137m per skein

11 (12, 13, 14, 16) skeins, Off White (#0002)

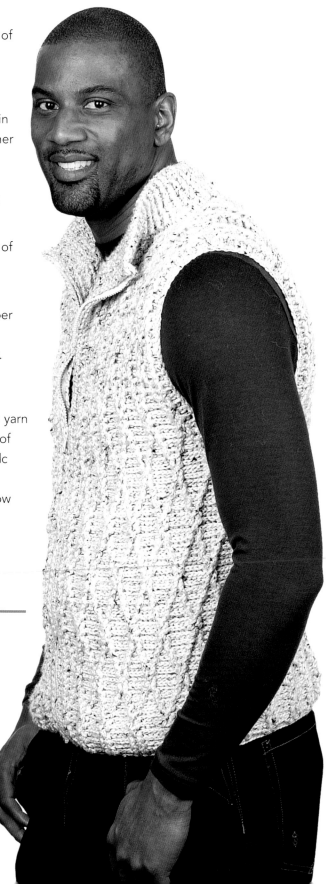

The Sport of Crochet

The combination of cotton yarn and a mesh-like stitch pattern helped me create this jersey. It's perfect for a good workout or for brunch at that neighborhood restaurant you've been meaning to try.

Skill Level
Experienced

Finished Size
Sizes: S (M, L, XL, XXL): 38 (40, 42, 44, 46)"/96.5 (101.5, 106.5, 112, 117)cm
Sweater shown in size L.

You Will Need
Color A: 1335 (1583, 1634, 1715, 1878)yd/1221 (1448, 1494, 1568, 1718)m of (4) medium weight cotton yarn, in green
Color B: 504 (505, 505, 517, 544)yd/461 (463, 463, 473, 498)m of (4) medium weight cotton yarn, in black
Hook: 6.50mm (size K-10½ U.S.) (or size to obtain gauge)
Stitch marker
Yarn needle

Stitches Used
Chain stitch (ch)
Single crochet (sc)
Slip stitch (sl st)

Gauge
15 sts x 8 rows = 4"/10cm in pattern stitch of Panel C
Always take time to check your gauge.

Instructions

Pattern Stitch

Ch required number of sts.

Row 1 (RS): Sc in 2nd ch from hook, *ch 1, sk next ch, sc in next ch; rep from * across, turn.

Row 2: Ch 1, sc in 1st sc, sc in next ch-1 sp *ch 1, sc in next ch-1 space; rep from * across to last ch-1 sp, sc in last sc, turn.

Row 3: Ch 1, sc in 1st sc, *ch 1, sc in next ch-1 sp; rep from * across to last ch-1 sp, ch 1, sc in last sc, turn.

Rep rows 2–3 for pattern stitch.

Back

With A, ch 72 (76, 84, 86, 92).

Work in pattern stitch until piece measures 22 (23, 24, 24½, 25½)"/56 (58.5, 61, 62, 65)cm from beg—71 (75, 83, 85, 91) sts.

SHAPE FIRST SHOULDER

Next row: Work in pattern stitch as established across 1st 25 (25, 25, 27, 27) sts, turn, leaving rem sts unworked.

Work even in pattern stitch until piece measures 23 (24, 25, 25½, 26½)"/58.5 (61, 63.5, 65, 67.5)cm from beg. Fasten off.

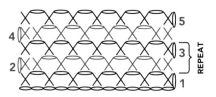

Fig. 1: Pattern stitch

SHAPE SECOND SHOULDER

Next row: Sk 21 (25, 33, 31, 37) sts to the left of last st made in 1st row of first shoulder, join A in next st, starting in same st, work in pattern stitch across, turn—25 (25, 25, 27, 27) sts.

Work even in pattern stitch until piece measures 23 (24, 25, 25½, 26½)"/58.5 (61, 63.5, 65, 67.5)cm from beg. Fasten off.

Front

Work same as back until piece measures 18 (19, 20, 20½, 21½)"/45.5 (48.5, 51, 52, 54.5)cm from beg. Place stitch marker in center st of last row.

SHAPE FIRST SHOULDER

Next row: Maintaining pattern stitch as established, work across, working sc in last st before stitch marker, turn, leaving rem sts unworked—35 (37, 40, 42, 45) sts.

Maintaining pattern stitch, work even until piece measures 23 (24, 25, 25½, 26½)"/58.5 (61, 63.5, 65, 67.5)cm from beg. Fasten off.

SHAPE SECOND SHOULDER

Next row: Join A in 1st st to the right of stitch marker, ch 1, sc in same st, work in pattern st across, turn—35 (37, 40, 42, 45) sts.

Maintaining pattern stitch, work even until piece measures 23 (24, 25, 25½, 26½)"/58.5 (61, 63.5, 65, 67.5)cm from beg. Fasten off.

SIDE EDGING

Row 1: With RS facing, join A with a sc to 1st st on one long edge of front, *ch 1, skip 1 row, sc in end of next row; rep from * across, ending with sc in last row. Fasten off.

Rep side edging on other long edge of front and on ea long edge of back.

Side Panels

Work the following to create the side panels on each edge of both front and back (the black area under the armholes).

Place a marker 15 (15½, 16, 16, 16½)"/38 (39.5, 40.5, 40.5, 42)cm above bottom edge on both side edges of both front and back.

FIRST SIDE PANEL

Row 1: With WS facing, join B with a sc in 1st st on left side edge of front, work even in pattern across to marker, turn, leaving rem sts unworked.

Work even in pattern stitch until side panel measures 2½"/6.5cm from beg. Fasten off.

With RS facing, rep first side panel across right side edge of front.

Rep side panel on 2 sides of back.

Sleeve Half (make 4)

With A, ch 20.

Work even in pattern stitch for 4 rows.

Note: All increases will be worked on one side of sleeve half while other edge will be straight.

Inc 1 st at beg of next row and every 4th row thereafter until 41 (43, 45, 47, 49) sts are on work, then work even until piece measures 20½ (22, 23½, 25, 26½)"/52 (56, 59.5, 63.5, 67.5)cm from beg. Fasten off.

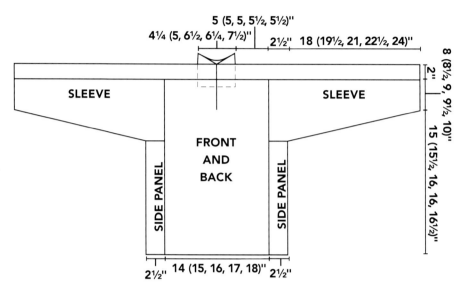

Fig. 2: Sweater diagram

Sleeve Trim

Row 1: With RS facing, join A with a sc in 1st st on straight edge of one sleeve, *ch 1, skip next row, sc in end of next row; rep from * across to end of sleeve. Fasten off.

Rep sleeve trim on ea of 3 rem sleeve halves.

Set in sleeve pieces into the notch created by the side panels, and whipstitch into place.

Top Panel

Row 1: Join B with sc in first st in top edge of front right shoulder, work in pattern stitch across shoulder, then across top edge of sleeve, turn. Work even in pattern stitch for 4 more rows. Fasten off.

Rep top panel across top edge of left side of front and left sleeve. In same manner, rep top panel across left shoulder of back and left sleeve. Rep top panel across right shoulder of back and right sleeve.

Assemble

With RS facing, using B, sew shoulders, tops of sleeves, and sides. With A, sew bottom sleeve seams.

Finishing

COLLAR

Row 1: With RS facing, join B with a sc in 1st row on top of top panel on right side of back neck, work in pattern stitch across right side of neck edge, across back neck edge, and up left side of neck edge, sc in next st on top edge of front, turn.

Row 2: Work in pattern stitch across back neck edge, sc in next st on top edge of front, turn.

Rep row 2 until all rem sts on top edge of front are worked. Fasten off.

Weave in ends.

Yarn Used

Nashua Handknits Cilantro, 70% cotton/30% polyester, 1¾oz/50g = 136yd/125m per skein

(A) 10 (12, 12, 13, 14) skeins, Lime Sorbet (#012)

(B) 4 skeins, Black (#002)

Convertible Cover

As I was designing this afghan square, I realized that the back looked just as fantastic as the front! By alternating the squares in a checkerboard pattern, there is no right or wrong side to this throw.

Skill Level
Intermediate

Finished Size
42 x 54"/106.5 x 137cm

You Will Need
Color A: 450yd/411m of (6) super bulky weight yarn
Color B: 300yd/274m of (6) super bulky weight yarn
Color C: 250yd/229m of (6) super bulky weight yarn
Hook: 6.50mm (size K-10½ U.S.) (or size to obtain gauge)
Yarn needle

Stitches Used
Chain stitch (ch)
Double crochet (dc)
Front post double crochet (FPdc)
Slip stitch (sl st)

Special Stitches
Reverse single crochet (reverse sc): Working from left to right, insert hook from front to back through next st to the right, yo, draw yarn though st, yo, draw yarn through 2 lps on hook.
V-stitch (V-st): (Dc, ch 1, dc) in same st or sp.

Gauge
7 sts x 5 rows = 4"/10cm in dc; first 2 rnds of motif = 4½"/11.5cm in diameter; motif = 12"/30.5cm square
Always take time to check your gauge.

Instructions

Motif (make 12)

With B, ch 4, join with sl st to form a ring.

Rnd 1 (RS): Ch 5 (counts as dc, ch 2), (3 dc in ring, ch 2) three times, 2 dc in ring, sl st to 3rd ch of beginning ch-5 to join.

Rnd 2: Sl st in next ch-2 sp, ch 5 (counts as dc, ch 2), 2 dc in same sp, *sk next dc, V-st in next dc, sk next dc**, (2 dc, ch 2, 2 dc) in corner ch-2 sp; rep from * around, ending last rep at **, dc in corner sp, sl st in 3rd ch of beginning ch-5 to join. Fasten off.

With RS facing, join A with sl st in any corner ch-2 sp.

Rnd 3: Ch 3, (dc, ch 2, 2 dc) in same sp, *sk next dc, FPdc in next dc, V-st in next ch-1 sp, sk next dc, FPdc in next dc, sk next dc**, (2 dc, ch 2, 2 dc) in corner sp; rep from * around, ending last rep at **, sl st in top of beginning ch-3 to join. Fasten off.

With RS facing, join C with sl st in any corner ch-2 sp.

Rnd 4: Ch 3, (dc, ch 2, 2 dc) in same sp, *sk next dc, FPdc in each of next 2 sts, V-st in next ch-1 sp, sk next dc, FPdc in each of next 2 sts, sk next dc**, (2 dc, ch 2, 2 dc) in corner ch-2 sp; rep from * around, ending last rep at **, sl st in top of beginning ch-3 to join. Fasten off.

With RS facing, join A with sl st in any corner ch-2 sp.

Rnd 5: Ch 3, (dc, ch 2, 2 dc) in same sp, *sk next dc, FPdc in each of next 3 sts, V-st in next ch-1 sp, sk next dc, FPdc in each of next 3 sts, sk next dc**, (2 dc, ch 2, 2 dc) in corner ch-2 sp; rep from * around, ending last rep at **, sl st in top of beginning ch-3 to join. Fasten off.

With RS facing, join B with sl st in any corner ch-2 sp.

Rnd 6: Ch 3, (dc, ch 2, 2 dc) in same sp, *sk next dc, FPdc in each of next 4 sts, V-st in next ch-1 sp, sk next dc, FPdc in each of next 4 sts, sk next dc**, (2 dc, ch 2, 2 dc) in corner ch-2 sp; rep from * around, ending last rep at **, sl st in top of beginning ch-3 to join. Fasten off.

With RS facing, join A with sl st in any corner ch-2 sp.

Rnd 7: Ch 3, (dc, ch 2, 2 dc) in same sp, *sk next dc, FPdc in each of next 5 sts, V-st in next ch-1 sp, sk next dc, FPdc in each of next 5 sts, sk next dc**, (2 dc, ch 2, 2 dc) in corner ch-2 sp; rep from * around, ending last rep at **, sl st in top of beginning ch-3 to join. Fasten off.

With RS facing, join C with sc in any corner ch-2 sp.

Rnd 8: Work 2 more sc in same sp, *sc in BL only of each st across to next corner**, 3 sc in corner ch-2 sp; rep from * around, ending last rep at **, sl st to first sc to join. Fasten off.

Assemble

Lay out afghan in three strips of four squares each. Alternate RS and WS facing up in a checkerboard pattern. Use C to whipstitch squares together.

Finishing

Weave in all ends, being sure to hide them well so that they are not visible on either side of the afghan.

AFGHAN BORDER

With either side facing, join C with sl st in 2nd sc of any corner.

Rnd 1: Ch 3, (dc, ch 2, 2 dc) in same st, *dc in each st across to next corner sc**, (2 dc, ch 2, 2 dc) in corner sc; rep from * around, ending last rep at **, sl st in top of beginning ch 3 to join. Fasten off.

With same side facing, join A with sl st in any corner ch-2 sp.

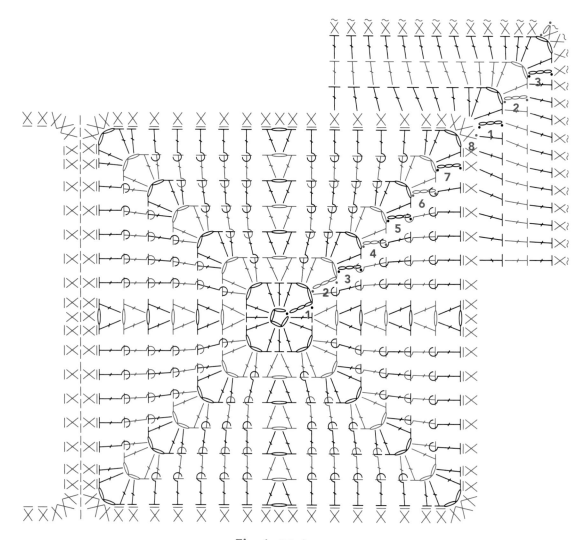

Fig. 1: Stitch pattern

Rnd 2: Ch 3, (dc, ch 2, 2 dc) in same sp, *dc in each st across to next corner ch-2 sp**, (2 dc, ch 2, 2 dc) in corner ch-2 sp; rep from * around, ending last rep at **, sl st in top of beginning ch 3 to join. Fasten off.

Rnd 3: With B, rep rnd 2.

With same side facing, join A with sl st in any corner ch-2 sp.

Rnd 4: Ch 1, reverse sc in each st around, working 2 reverse sc in each corner ch-2 sp, sl st to first sc to join. Fasten off. Weave in ends.

Yarn Used

Caron Simply Soft Quick, 100% acrylic, 3 oz/85g = 50yd/46m per skein

(A) 9 skeins, White (#0001)

(B) 6 skeins, Berry Blue (#0015)

(C) 5 skeins, Dark Sage (#0006)

Vestatility

Going to the office? Throw on this vest. Going out on a date? Throw on this vest. Your kid's soccer game? Say it with me: throw on this vest. You get the picture.

Skill Level
Experienced

Finished Size
Sizes: S (M, L, XL, XXL): 40 (42, 44, 46, 48)"/101.5 (106.5, 111.5, 117, 122)cm
Sweater shown in size L.

You Will Need
724 (791, 862, 915, 995)yd/662 (724, 788, 837, 910)m of (**4**) medium weight yarn, in brown
Hook: 3.75mm (size F-5 U.S.) (*or size to obtain gauge*)
Stitch marker
Yarn needle

Stitches Used
Back post double crochet (BPdc)
Chain stitch (ch)
Double crochet (dc)
Front post double crochet (FPdc)
Single crochet (sc)
Slip stitch (sl st)

Special Stitches
Single crochet two together (sc2tog):
(Insert hook in next st, yo, draw yarn through st) twice, yo, draw yarn through 3 lps on hk.
Double crochet two together (dc2tog): (Yo, insert hook in next st, yo, draw yarn through st, yo, draw yarn through 2 lps on hk) twice, yo, draw yarn through 3 lps on hook.
Front post double crochet 3 together (FPdc3tog): (Yo, insert hook from back to front to back again around the post of designated st, yo, draw yarn through st, yo, draw yarn through 2 lps on hook) 3 times, yo, draw yarn through 4 lps on hook.

Gauge
15 sts x 13 rows = 4"/10cm in pattern stitch
Always take time to check your gauge.

Instructions

1 x 1 Ribbing Pattern

Row 1 (WS): Ch 3 (counts as dc), dc evenly across, turn.

Row 2: Ch 2 (counts as hdc), *FPdc around the post of next st, BPdc around the post of next st; rep from * across to within last st, hdc in last st, turn.

Pattern Stitch

Ch required number of sts.

Row 1: Ch 1, sc in 1st st, dc in next st, *sc in next st, dc in next st; rep from * across, turn.

Row 2: Ch 3 (counts as dc), sc in next sc, *dc in next dc, sc in next sc; rep from * across, turn.

Row 3: Ch 1, sc in first sc, dc in next dc, *sc in next sc, dc in next dc; rep from * across, turn.

Repeat rows 2-3 for pattern.

Back

Ch 76 (80, 84, 88, 92).

Work in 1 x 1 ribbing pattern—74 (78, 82, 86, 90) sts.

Work even in pattern stitch until piece measures 15 (15½, 16, 16, 16½)"/38 (39.5, 40.5, 40.5, 42)cm from beg.

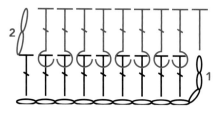

Fig. 1: 1 x 1 ribbing pattern

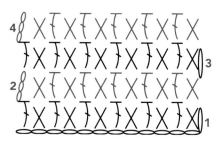

Fig. 2: Pattern stitch

SHAPE ARMHOLES

Cont in stitch pattern dec 1 st at end of next 10 rows—64 (68, 72, 76, 80) sts at end of last row. Work even in pattern stitch until piece measures 24 (25, 26, 26½, 27½)"/61 (63.5, 66, 67.5, 70)cm from beg. Fasten off.

Note: The decrease used is determined by what the last st of the row is. When you come to the end of the row and the last st would be a sc, dc2tog to create the decrease. If the last st would be a dc, sc2tog to create the decrease.

Front

Work same as back until piece
measures 15 (15½, 16, 16,
16½)"/38 (39.5, 40.5, 40.5, 42)cm
from beg. Place stitch marker
in center of current row, begin
working armhole shaping as for
back, and at the same time begin
working V-neck shaping as follows.

SHAPE FIRST FRONT

Next row: Work in stitch pattern
across to within 2 sts of st marker,
dec 1 st in next 2 sts, turn, leaving
rem sts unworked. Work in pattern
stitch, dec 1 st at neck edge every
other row 12 (12, 13, 14, 15) times;
then dec 1 st at neck edge every row
0 (2, 2, 2, 1) times; then work even
in stitch pattern until piece measures
24 (25, 26, 26½, 27½)"/61 (63.5, 66,
67.5, 70)cm from beg. Fasten off.

SHAPE SECOND FRONT

Next row: Join yarn in first st to
the left of last st made in 1st row
of first front, maintaining pattern
stitch, dec 1 st at neck edge, then
work in pattern stitch across, turn.
Work same as First Front, reversing
shaping. Fasten off.

Assemble

Sew shoulder seams. Sew
side seams.

105

Finishing

V-NECK RIBBING

Rnd 1: With WS facing, join yarn at shoulder seam on neck edge, ch-3 (counts as dc), dc evenly around, being sure that you work 1 dc at the point of the V, and being sure that you end with an even number of stitches, sl st in 3rd ch of beg ch-3 to join, turn.

Rnd 2: Ch 2, *FPdc in next st, BPdc in next st; rep from * across to within 1 st of dc in the point of the V, FPdc3tog across next 3 sts, BPdc in next st, rep from * around to within last st, FPdc in next st, sl st in 2nd ch of beg ch-2 to join. Fasten off.

ARMHOLE RIBBING

Rnd 1: With WS facing, join yarn at underarm seam, ch 3 (counts as dc), dc evenly around, working an even number of stitches, sl st in 3rd ch of beg ch-3 to join, turn.

Rnd 2: Ch 2, *FPdc in next st, BPdc in next st; rep from * around to within last st, FPdc in next st, sl st in 2nd ch of beg ch-2 to join. Fasten off.

Weave in ends.

Yarn Used

Moda Dea Fashionista, 50% acrylic/50% Tencel/Lyocell, 3½oz/ 100g = 183yd/168m per skein

4 (5, 5, 5, 6) skeins, Milk Chocolate (#6140)

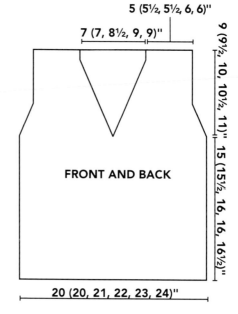

5 (5½, 5½, 6, 6)"

7 (7, 8½, 9, 9)"

9 (9½, 10, 10½, 11)"

15 (15½, 16, 16, 16½)"

FRONT AND BACK

20 (20, 21, 22, 23, 24)"

Fig. 3: **Front and back diagram**

Power Tie

Think about all the knitted or crocheted ties you've ever seen. Don't you wish they weren't so summer-camp-craft-class-looking? These ties use thread in amazing colors and a technique that produces a great design.

Skill Level
Experienced

Finished Size
58"/147.5cm long—one size fits
anyone

You Will Need
Color A: 300 yd/275m of (**0**) lace
weight (10-count bedspread
weight) cotton crochet thread
Color B: 300 yd/275m of (**0**) lace
weight (10-count bedspread
weight) cotton crochet thread
Color C: 100 yd/92m of (**0**) lace
weight (10-count bedspread
weight) cotton crochet thread
Hook: 1.50mm/8 steel crochet hook
(*or size to obtain gauge*)
Tapestry needle

Color A: Variegated light green/blue
Color B: Light green
Color C: White

Stitches Used
Chain stitch (ch)
Double crochet (dc)
Single crochet (sc)
Slip stitch (sl st)

Special Stitches
Single crochet two together
(sc2tog): (Insert hook in next st,
yo, draw yarn through st) twice,
yo, draw yarn through 3 lps on
hook.

Gauge
10 sts x 10 rows = 1"/2.5cm in sc
*Always take time to check your
gauge.*

Instructions

Note: *In the chart, read all odd-
numbered rows from right to left,
rep from A to B across. Work all
even-numbered rows from left
to right, rep from B to A across.
Always work a sc on first and
last st of row regardless of what
chart indicates. Edges will be
hemmed under.*

Tie

With Color C, ch 37.

Foundation row: Sc in 2nd ch
from hook and in each ch across,
turn—36 sc.

Next row: Ch 1, sc in each sc
across. Fasten off.

Work even following chart until
piece measures 2"/5cm from the
beg. Cont following chart, dec 1 st
(by working sc2tog) at beg and end
of next row and every 32 rows 9
times total—18 sts at end of
last row.

Work even on 18 sts following chart
until piece measures 58"/147.5cm
from beg. Fasten off.

Finishing

Weave in ends. Each long side
of the tie will need to be roll
hemmed, which is super easy, just
by inserting your hook through the
end stitch of a row, then counting
three stitches over on the same row
on the back side and inserting the
hook through the base of the stitch,
pull up thread and work a slip st.

Continue across entire edge, and
the sides will gently roll under to
create a finished look. With RS
tog, fold bottom end of Tie in half
lengthwise. With Color C, matching
sts of foundation ch, sew beg of
foundation ch to end of foundation
ch. Turn RS out.

Rep on top end of Tie.

Weave in ends.

Yarn Used

J&P Coats Royale Classic Crochet,
100% mercerized cotton, 350yd/
320m per ball

(A) 1 ball, 300yd/275m, Oasis
(#0928)

(B) 1 ball, 350yd/320m, Frosty
Green (#0661)

(C) 1 ball, 400yd/366m, White
(#0201)

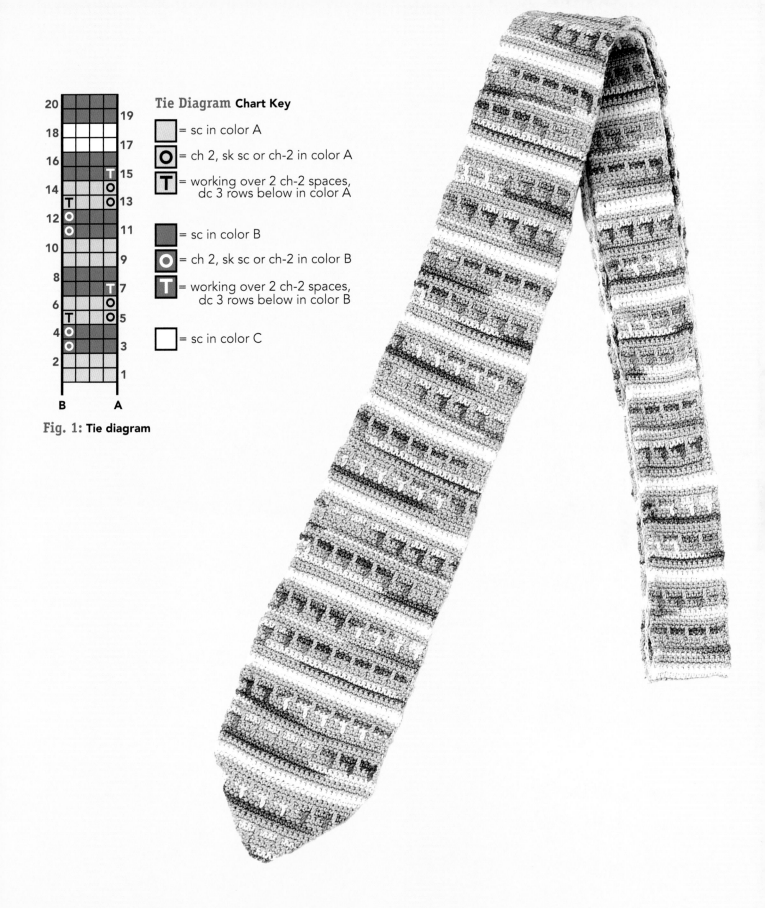

Tie Diagram **Chart Key**

☐ = sc in color A

Ⓞ = ch 2, sk sc or ch-2 in color A

Ⓣ = working over 2 ch-2 spaces,
dc 3 rows below in color A

■ = sc in color B

Ⓞ = ch 2, sk sc or ch-2 in color B

Ⓣ = working over 2 ch-2 spaces,
dc 3 rows below in color B

☐ = sc in color C

Fig. 1: Tie diagram

Cubana Cardigan

As I packed clothes for a vacation, I realized that most of the shirts I own have the cubana styling that inspired this sweater. Do I look like a tourist everywhere I go? Maybe—but a really sharply dressed one!

Instructions

Note: *Sweater is worked in panels from hem to shoulder, with ribbing worked into stitch pattern.*

Left Side Panels

Ch required number of sts.

Foundation row (RS): Sc in 2nd ch from hook and in each ch across, turn.

Row 1 (WS): Ch 1, sc in first 5 sts, hdc in each st across, turn.

Row 2 (RS): Ch 1, sc in BL only of each st across, turn.

Rep rows 1–2 for stitch pattern.

Skill Level
Experienced

Finished Size
Sizes: S (M, L, XL, XXL): 42 (44, 46, 48, 51)"/106.5 (112, 117, 122, 129.5)cm
Sweater shown in size M.

You Will Need
Color A: 1022 (1116, 1215, 1297, 1419)yd/935 (1021, 1111, 1186, 1298)m of (5) bulky weight yarn, in tan
Color B: 227 (248, 270, 288, 315)yd/208 (227, 247, 264, 288)m of (5) bulky weight yarn, in variegated colors
Hook: 5.50mm (size I-9 U.S.) (*or size to obtain gauge*)
Yarn needle
Four 1"/2.5cm buttons

Stitches Used
Chain stitch (ch)
Half double crochet (hdc)
Slip stitch (sl st)
Single crochet (sc)

Special Stitches

Single crochet two together (sc2tog): (Insert hook in next st, yo, draw yarn through st) twice, yo, draw yarn through 3 lps on hook.

Double crochet two together (dc2tog): (Yo, insert hook in next st, yo, draw yarn through st, yo, draw yarn through 2 lps on hook) twice, yo, draw yarn through 3 lps on hook.

Gauge

11 sts x 9 rows = 4"/10cm in stitch pattern

Always take time to check your gauge.

Right Side Panels

Ch required number of sts.

Foundation row (RS): Sc into 2nd ch from hook and into each ch across, turn.

Row 1 (WS): Ch 1, hdc in each st across to within last 5 sts, sc in last 5 sts, turn.

Row 2 (RS): Ch 1, sc in BL only of each st across, turn.

Rep rows 1–2 for stitch pattern.

Back

Back is worked in two panels.

LEFT BACK PANEL

With Color A, ch 74 (77, 79, 81, 83).

Work in left side panel stitch pattern on 73 (76, 78, 80, 82) sts until 18 (19, 21, 22, 23) rows have been completed from beg. Fasten off.

RIGHT BACK PANEL

With Color A, ch 74 (77, 79, 81, 83).

Work in right side panel stitch pattern on 73 (76, 78, 80, 82) sts until 18 (19, 21, 22, 23) rows have been completed from beg. Fasten off.

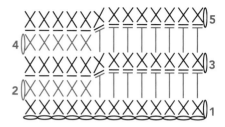

Fig. 1: Left side pattern

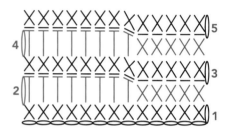

Fig. 2: Right side pattern

Front

LEFT FRONT PANEL

With Color B, ch 74 (77, 79, 81, 83).

Work in left side panel stitch pattern on 73 (76, 78, 80, 82) sts until 10 (11, 12, 13, 14) rows have been completed from beg. Fasten off B, join A. With Color A, work in left side panel stitch pattern until 18 (19, 21, 22, 23) rows have been completed from beg. Fasten off.

RIGHT FRONT PANEL

With Color B, ch 74 (77, 79, 81, 83).

Work in right side panel stitch pattern on 73 (76, 78, 80, 82) sts until 10 (11, 12, 13, 14) rows have been completed from beg. Fasten off B, join A. With Color A, work in left side panel stitch pattern until 18 (19, 21, 22, 23) rows have been completed from beg. Fasten off.

Sides

LEFT SIDE PANEL

With Color A, ch 49 (51, 53, 53, 53).

Work in left side panel stitch pattern on 48 (50, 52, 52, 52) sts until 10 rows have been completed from beg. Fasten off.

RIGHT SIDE PANEL

With Color A, ch 49 (51, 53, 53, 53).

Work in right side panel stitch pattern on 48 (50, 52, 52, 52) sts until 10 rows have been completed from beg. Fasten off.

Sleeve (make 2)

With Color A, ch 23 (27, 29, 29, 31).

Row 1: Sc in 2nd ch from hook and in each ch across, turn—22 (26, 28, 28, 30) sc.

Rows 2–4: Ch 1, sc in each st across, turn.

Row 5: Ch 1, hdc in each st across, turn.

Row 6 (RS): Ch 1, sc in BL only of each st across, turn.

Rep rows 5–6. Inc 1 st at ea end of every RS row until 44 (44, 50, 50, 56) sts are on work, then work even until sleeve measures 18½ (19, 19½, 20, 20½)"/47 (48.5, 49.5, 51, 52)cm from beg.

Begin sleeve cap.

Work in stitch pattern as established, dec 1 st at beg of next 1 (3, 0, 2, 0) rows, then dec 1 st at ea end of next 19 (18, 22, 21, 24) rows. Fasten off.

Assemble

With bottom ribbing aligned, sew left front and left side panels together according to chart; sew right front and right side panels together; sew back panels together. With RS facing, sew back to ea front across Color B sections. Sew side panels to back. Set in sleeves.

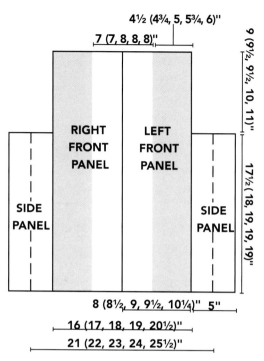

Fig. 3: Front and sides diagram

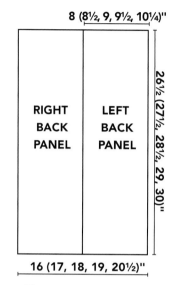

Fig. 4: Back diagram

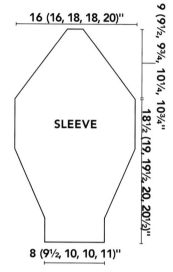

Fig. 5: Sleeve diagram

Finishing

COLLAR

Row 1: With RS facing, join Color A with a sc on neck edge at top of right-hand corner of right front panel, sc evenly across neckline to left-hand corner of left front, turn.

Row 2: Ch 1, hdc in each st across, turn.

Row 3: Ch 1, sc in BL only of each st across, turn.

Rows 4–7: Rep rows 2–3. Fasten off.

BUTTON BAND

Row 1: With RS facing, join Color A with a sc to bottom right-hand corner of right front, sc evenly across right front edge to corner of collar, turn.

Rows 2–3: Ch 1, sc in each sc across, turn. Fasten off.

BUTTONHOLE BAND

Row 1: With RS facing, join Color A with a sc on top left-hand corner of left front, sc evenly across left front edge to bottom corner, turn.

Row 2: Ch 1, sc in each of first 3 sc, *ch 2, sk next 2 sts, sc in each of next 11 sts; rep from * 3 times, sc in ea st across, turn.

Row 3: Ch 1, sc in ea sc across, working 2 sc in ea ch-2 sp. Fasten off.

Weave in ends.

Sew buttons to button band on right panel corresponding to buttonholes.

Yarn Used

Moda Dea Metro, 94% acrylic/6% nylon, 3½oz/100g = 124yd/114m per skein

(A) 9 (9, 10, 11, 12) skeins, Wheat (#9321)

(B) 2 (2, 3, 3, 3) skeins, Ivy League (#9940)

Finale Argyle

When it comes to color for guys, it gets tricky. A dude can only handle so much. Here is my version of the classic argyle with just enough color to make it interesting without going overboard.

Skill Level
Experienced

Finished Size
Sizes: S (M, L, XL, XXL): 41 (43, 45, 47, 49)"/104 (109, 114.5, 119.5, 124.5)cm

Sweater shown in size L.

You Will Need
Color A: 1598 (1763, 1969, 2062, 2239)yd/1462 (1612, 1800, 1886, 2048)m of (4) medium weight yarn, in gray

Color B: 218 (218, 218, 218, 218)yd/200 (200, 200, 200, 200)m of (4) medium weight yarn, in turquoise

Color C: 218 (218, 218, 218, 218)yd/200 (200, 200, 200, 200)m of (4) medium weight yarn, in brown

Color D: 218 (218, 218, 218, 218)yd/200 (200, 200, 200, 200)m of (4) medium weight yarn, in dark orange

Hook: 3.75mm (size F-5 U.S.) (*or size to obtain gauge*)

Yarn needle

Stitches Used
Back post double crochet (BPdc)
Chain stitch (ch)
Double crochet (dc)
Front post double crochet (FPdc)
Slip stitch (sl st)

Instructions

Note: Unless otherwise indicated, entire sweater is worked in single crochet.

1 x 1 Ribbing Pattern

Ch required number of sts.

Row 1: Dc in 4th ch from hook and in ea ch across, turn.

Row 2: Ch 2 (counts as hdc), *FPdc around the post of next st, BPdc around the post of next st; rep from * across to within last st, hdc in last st, turn.

Rep row 2 for pattern.

Back

With A, ch 84 (88, 92, 96, 100).

Work in 1 x 1 ribbing pattern for 2 rows—82 (86, 90, 94, 98) sts.

Work even in sc until piece measures 15 (15½, 16, 16, 16½)"/38 (39.5, 40.5, 40.5, 42)cm from beg.

SHAPE ARMHOLES

Next row: Ch 1, sc in each st across to within last 9 sts, turn, leaving rem sts unworked—73 (77, 81, 85, 89) sc.

Next row: Rep last row—64 (68, 72, 76, 80) sts.

Work even in sc until piece measures 23 (24, 25, 25½,

26½)"/58.5 (61, 63.5, 65, 67.5)cm from beg, ending with a WS row.

SHAPE RIGHT SHOULDER

Next row: Ch 1, sc in each of first 16 (18, 20, 22, 24) sts, turn, leaving rem sts unworked. Work even in sc until piece measures 24 (25, 26, 26½, 27½)"/61 (63.5, 66, 67.5, 70)cm from beg. Fasten off.

SHAPE LEFT SHOULDER

Next row: With RS facing, sk 32 sts to the left of last st made in first row of right shoulder, join A in next st, ch 1, starting in same st, sc in each st across—16 (18, 20, 22, 24) sts, turn. Work even in sc until piece measures 24 (25, 26, 26½, 27½)"/61 (63.5, 66, 67.5, 70)cm from beg. Fasten off.

Front

Work in sc, following a chart. To follow the chart, work all odd-numbered rows from right to left; work all even-numbered rows from left to right. To change color, complete last sc of first color with next color, drop first color to wrong side to be picked up in next row. Do not carry colors across; attach a separate ball of yarn for each new color section.

With A, ch 84 (88, 92, 96, 100).

Work in 1 x 1 ribbing pattern for 2 rows—82 (86, 90, 94, 98) sts.

Special Stitches

Single crochet two together (sc2tog): (Insert hook in next st, yo, draw yarn through st) twice, yo, draw yarn through 3 lps on hook.

Front post double crochet 3 together (FPdc3tog): (Yo, insert hook from back to front to back again around the post of designated st, yo, draw yarn through st, yo, draw yarn through 2 lps on hook) 3 times, yo, draw yarn through 4 lps on hook.

Gauge

16 sts x 18 rows = 4"/10cm in sc
Always take time to check your gauge.

Row 1: Ch 1, sc in each st across, following chart for color changes.

Work even in sc following chart for color changes until piece measures 15 (15½, 16, 16, 16½)"/38 (39.5, 40.5, 40.5, 42)cm from beg.

SHAPE ARMHOLES

Next row: Ch 1, maintaining color pattern as established, sc in each st across to within last 9 sts, turn, leaving rem sts unworked—73 (77, 81, 85, 89) sc.

Next row: Rep last row—64 (68, 72, 76, 80) sts.

Maintaining color pattern, work even in sc until piece measures 16 (17, 18, 18½, 19½)"/40.5 (43, 45.5, 47, 49.5)cm from beg, ending with a WS row.

SHAPE RIGHT FRONT

Next row: Ch 1, maintaining color pattern as established, sc in each of first 32 (34, 36, 38, 40) sts, turn, leaving rem sts unworked.

Maintaining color pattern as established, dec 1 sc at neck edge on every other row 16 times—16 (18, 20, 22, 24) sts at end of last row.

Maintaining color pattern, work even in sc until piece measures 24 (25, 26, 26½, 27½)"/61 (63.5, 66, 67.5, 70)cm from beg. Fasten off.

SHAPE LEFT FRONT

Next row: With RS facing, referring to chart, join appropriate color in first st to the left of last st made in first row of right front, ch 1, maintaining color pattern as established, sc in each st across— 32 (34, 36, 38, 40) sc.

Maintaining color pattern as established, dec 1 st at neck edge of next row and every other row for a total of 16 times—16 (18, 20, 22, 24) sts at end of last row.

Maintaining color pattern, work even in sc until piece measures 24 (25, 26, 26½, 27½)"/61 (63.5, 66, 67.5, 70)cm from beg. Fasten off.

Sleeve (make 2)

With A, ch 38 (42, 44, 46, 46).

Work in 1 x 1 ribbing pattern for 2 rows—36 (40, 42, 44, 44) sc.

Work 2 rows even in sc. Then, inc 1 st at beg and end of next row and every 4th row until 60 (64, 72, 72, 80) sts are on work; then work even until sleeve measures 18½ (19, 19½, 20, 20½)"/47 (48.5, 49.5, 51, 52)cm from beg.

SHAPE SLEEVE CAP

Dec 1 st at end of next 16 (16, 12, 16, 12) rows; then dec 1 st at beg and end of next 20 (22, 28, 26, 32) rows—4 sts. Fasten off.

Assemble

Sew shoulder seams. Set in sleeves. Sew sleeve and side seams.

Finishing

NECK EDGING

Rnd 1: With WS facing, join A along back of neckline, ch 3 (counts as dc), dc evenly around neck opening, being sure that you work one dc at the point of the V, and being sure that you end with an even number of stitches, sl st in top of beg ch-3, turn.

Rnd 2 (RS): Ch 2, *FPdc in next st, BPdc in next st; rep from * around to within one st of dc in the point of the V, FPdc3tog in next 3 sts, rep from * to * around, sl st in top of beg ch-3. Fasten off.

Weave in ends.

Yarn Used

South West Trading Company's Karaoke, 50% Soysilk/50% wool, 1¾oz/50g = 109yd/100m per skein

(A) 15 (17, 18, 19, 21) skeins, Taupe (#301)

(B) 2 skeins, Mermaid (#288)

(C) 2 skeins, Rustica (#281)

(D) 2 skeins, Tobacco (#292)

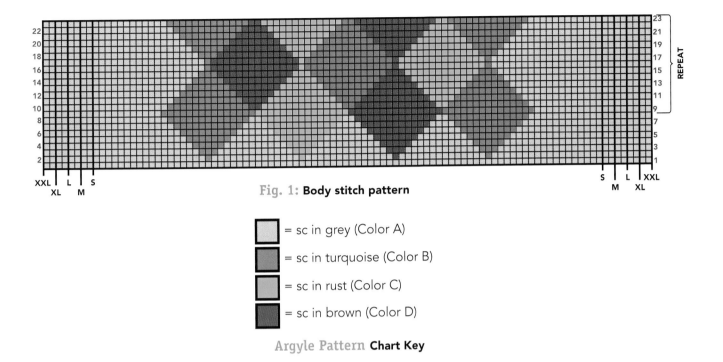

Fig. 1: **Body stitch pattern**

☐ = sc in grey (Color A)

☐ = sc in turquoise (Color B)

☐ = sc in rust (Color C)

☐ = sc in brown (Color D)

Argyle Pattern **Chart Key**

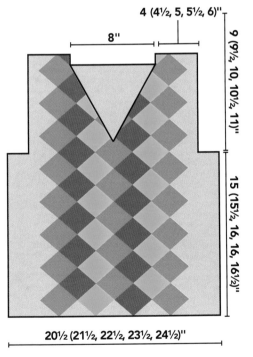

4 (4½, 5, 5½, 6)"

8"

9 (9½, 10, 10½, 11)"

15 (15½, 16, 16, 16½)"

20½ (21½, 22½, 23½, 24½)"

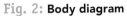

Fig. 2: **Body diagram**

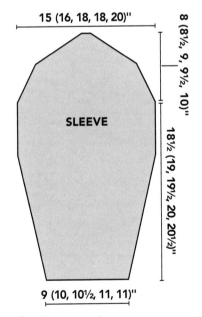

15 (16, 18, 18, 20)"

8 (8½, 9, 9½, 10)"

SLEEVE

18½ (19, 19½, 20, 20½)"

9 (10, 10½, 11, 11)"

Fig. 3: **Sleeve diagram**

Crochet Abbreviation Chart

This table lists the common crochet abbreviations used in the project instructions.

Abbreviation	Description
"	inch(es)
()	repeat the instructions in the parentheses the number of times specified
*	repeat the instructions after the * as instructed
beg	begin(ning)
BL	back loop(s)
BPdc	back post double crochet
BPdc2tog	back post double crochet two together
BPdc3tog	back post double crochet three together
Cbl-A	cable A
Cbl-B	cable B
Cbl-C	cable C
Cbl-D	cable D
ch(s)	chain(s)
cm	centimeter(s)
cont	continue
dc	double crochet(s)
dc2tog	double crochet two together
dc3tog	double crochet three together
dec	decrease/decreasing
dtr	double treble

Abbreviation	Description
ea	each
FL	front loop(s)
FPdc	front post double crochet
FPdc2tog	front post double crochet two together
FPdc3tog	front post double crochet three together
FPdtr	front post double treble crochet
FPtr	front post treble crochet
g	gram(s)
hdc	half double crochet(s)
hk	hook
inc	increase/increasing
lp(s)	loop(s)
m	meter(s)
mm	millimeter(s)
oz	ounce(s)
pbdc	piggyback double crochet
rem	remain(ing)
rep	repeat(ing)
rnd(s)	round(s)
RS	right side(s)
sc	single crochet(s)

Abbreviation	Description
sc2tog	single crochet two together
sk	skip
sl st	slip stitch(es)
sp	space
st(s)	stitch(es)
tr	treble crochet(s), sometimes called triple crochet
V-st	V-stitch
WS	wrong side(s)
X-st	crossed double crochet
yd	yard(s)
yo	yarn over hook

US vs. UK Crochet Terms

US	UK
chain (ch)	chain (ch)
single crochet (sc)	double crochet (dc)
double crochet (dc)	treble (tr)
half double crochet (hdc)	half treble (htr)
triple crochet (trc)	double treble (dtr)
slip stitch (sl st)	slip stitch (sl st)

Standard Yarn Weight System

Yarn Weight Symbol & Category Names	0	1	2	3	4	5	6
Types of Yarns in Category	Fingering, 10-count crochet thread	Sock, Fingering, Baby	Sport, Baby	DK, Light Worsted	Worsted, Afghan, Aran	Chunky, Craft, Rug	Bulky, Roving

Source: Craft Yarn Council of America's www.YarnStandards.com

Crochet Hook Sizes Chart

Yarn Hooks

US Size	Metric Size
B-1	2.25 mm
C-2	2.75 mm
C-3	3.25 mm
E-4	3.50 mm
F-5	3.75 mm
G-6	4.00 mm
7	4.50 mm
H-8	5.00 mm
I-9	5.50 mm
J-10	6.00 mm
K-10½	6.50 mm
L-11	8.00 mm
M/N-13	9.00 mm
N/P-15	10.00 mm

Steel Hooks

US Size	Metric Size
00	3.50 mm
0	3.25 mm
1	2.75 mm
2	2.25 mm
3	2.10 mm
4	2.00 mm
5	1.90 mm
6	1.80 mm
7	1.65 mm
8	1.50 mm
9	1.40 mm
10	1.30 mm
11	1.10 mm
12	1.00 mm
13	0.85 mm
14	0.75 mm

Stitch Key

— =Worked in front loop only

— =Worked in back loop only

Symbol	Stitch	Symbol	Stitch
⬭	Chain stitch (ch)		Back post dc (BPdc)
•	Slip stitch (sl st)		Front post tr (FPtr)
X	Single crochet (sc)		Back post tr (BPtr)
T	Half double crochet (hdc)		front post dtr (FPdtr)
T	Double crochet (dc)		Front post dc two together (FPdc2tog)
T	Treble crochet (tr)		Back post dc two together (BPdc2tog)
X̃	Reverse sc	X	Crossed dc (X-st)
	Front post dc (FPdc)	V	V-st

Crochet Stitches & Techniques

Whether you're new to the art of crochet or an experienced hand at it, here's your go-to guide for the techniques you'll need to know. It starts with a beginning guide (or refresher course) on the most common stitches.

Chain Stitch

The foundation for every crochet project is a length of chain stitches (chs). You crochet the rows—also called rounds (rnds)—of your project on top of this foundation chain.

Fig. 1: **Chain stitch**

Single Crochet

Single crochet (sc) is a short, basic stitch that creates a firm fabric and can watch the game uninterrupted. Wait, that's a single dude. The sc stitch is great for projects that need to be durable, and you can make this easy stitch with just a few steps.

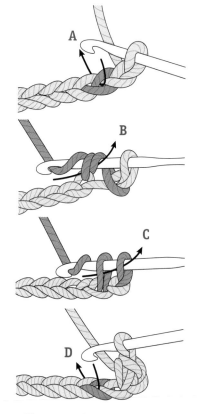

Figs. 2a–d: **Single crochet**

Double Crochet

Since the double crochet (dc) is nearly twice as tall as a single crochet (sc), you'll speed through projects quicker when they are made with this basic stitch. You'll find, though, that the resulting

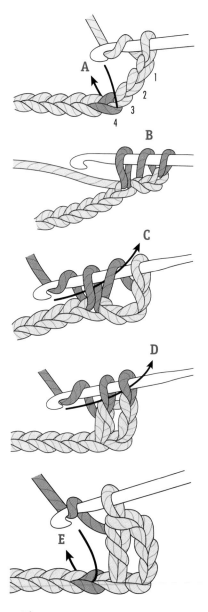

Figs. 3a–e: **Double crochet**

fabric is not as sturdy. The dc stitch is better suited to clothing you want to be soft and bendy, "bendy" being the technical term.

The Weekend Turtleneck project on page 68 shows how you can make a sweater quickly using this fantastic stitch.

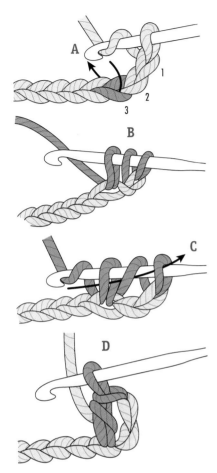

Figs. 4a–d: Half double crochet

Half Double Crochet

I love the half double crochet (hdc) and use it as often as possible. It's a bit smaller than the double crochet (dc) and a bit taller than the single crochet (sc), but it has an interesting texture to it on both the front and the back of the stitch. Give it a shot.

Check out the cool texture that I created on the Cubana Cardigan (page 110) by showing the backside of the hdc stitch.

Treble Crochet

We're talking some serious height here. Can you see the pattern forming? Each stitch is taller than the last, but the basic motions are

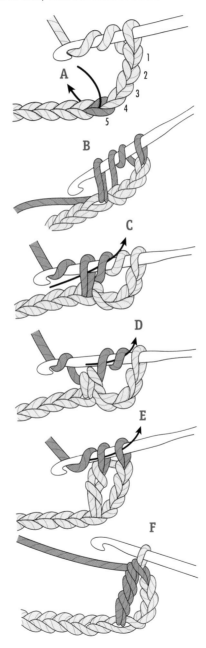

Figs. 5a–f: Treble crochet

the same. You'll see that I've used the treble (tr) stitch several different ways throughout the book.

Treble crochet stitches are fantastic for getting the job done quickly, for cool stitch combos, and even for creating a cabling look. You can see how that makes a great project with the To Aran Is Human cardigan on page 51.

Slip Stitch

I've saved the slip stitch (sl st) for last—even though it's the shortest stitch you'll make—because it is a multifunctional stitch (st) you can't live without...kind of like pizza, the remote control, or a well-stocked fridge, or in my case, hand sanitizer (but that's a whole other issue for a whole other book). You can use this stitch to create a firm, finished

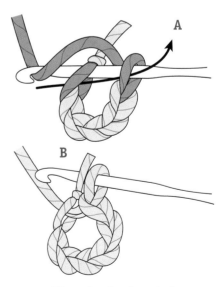

Figs. 6a–b: Slip stitch

edge or to join two finished crocheted pieces. You can also use it to join one end of a foundation chain to the opposite end, to create a ring that then forms the foundation for working pieces in the round.

Turning Your Work

When you reach the end of a row, you'll turn your work over to start the next row. But before you do, you'll need to make a turning chain (ch). Fortunately (because I'm always thinking ahead), I've written the number of chain stitches required right into the pattern.

Back Away from the Stitches

Actually, look closely at the fabric you're creating. Crocheted fabric is composed of stitches and spaces of varying sizes. A completed stitch has the front loop, the back loop, and the post. And spaces are usually created by chain stitches in between taller stitches.

As you work a crochet pattern, you may be directed to work into or around different parts of a stitch or even into the spaces between stitches. These subtle differences in working methods change the look of the stitch and the finished crochet fabric. Listed below are my two favorite ways to get a great texture into the fabric just by changing where you insert the hook to make the next stitch.

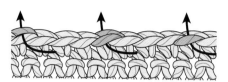

Fig. 7: **Back and front loops**

Back and Front Loops

As a general rule, you work a stitch into both top loops of your stitching row—doing so gives you a smooth fabric, and this is by far the most commonly used method. But you can do a little magic just by inserting a hook into only the front loop (FL) or back loop (BL) of a stitch, creating a fabric with a ribbed or ridged look.

For a great example of this technique, see the Baffy Buddies project on page 31. I'll give you specific instructions in the pattern if you need to work into front or back loops.

Back and Front Post

To me, this is the most exciting way to crochet. I use post stitches throughout this book. With post stitches, you can create raised patterns resembling ribbing or even intricate cables. They also make the fabric softer and much more bendy (there I go with the technical terms again). The way you insert your hook around a post—back post (BP) or front post (FP)—determines the look of the stitch.

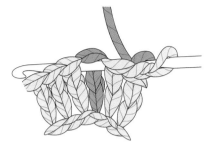

Fig. 8: **Back post**

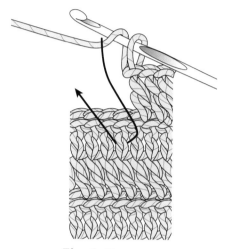

Fig. 9: **Front post**

Again, I'll give you specific instructions in the pattern if you need to use this technique to create a stitch. You can see how I used front and back post stitches to create texture and cabling on page 90 with the Zip It Cabled Vest.

Add Some Pizzazz (or Some Pizza—Your Choice)

Changing colors within a project is a great way to add your personality. If you swap between dark and light colors, you'll add bold attention-grabbing contrast that adds a lot of punch. If you swap between colors with similar qualities, you'll add subtle depth and texture to the project. Many yarn manufacturers produce several shades of the same color. Just by alternating between them, you can create a one-of-a-kind project, saving yourself that awkward moment at the hardware store where you run into some other dude wearing the same sweater.

Changing Colors or Threads

If you run out of thread or want to change colors or yarns while you're working, never join a new thread with a knot—it's messy, it's not effective, and it could very well lead to a fiber disaster. Whenever possible, work in a new strand of yarn at the end of a row. If you notice your yarn diminishing or if you think you might not have enough to finish another row, don't be afraid to pull out the row and start over, attaching a new ball of yarn. Sacrifice that yard of yarn because, in the long run, your project will be better for it.

Multiple Color Management (or MCM)

When a project calls for several areas with different colors, wind small amounts of each color onto a bobbin and hold it to the back of the fabric. (Bobbins are simply little pieces of cardboard to hold small amounts of yarn wrapped around them.) Change colors as indicated in the previous section, following the pattern closely. By keeping the yarn on bobbins, you eliminate the risk of getting them all tangled together. The Finale Argyle sweater on page 115 shows how dynamic a project can look in multiple colors.

Gauge Gauge Gauge

No matter how much you're jonesing to get started, you must check your gauge or the project will turn out small enough for your Chihuahua or big enough for the whole team. Say it with me once and for all: Hook size matters! At the beginning of every pattern, you'll find a gauge specified for the design. Measure your gauge to be sure that you're using the correct hook size. Pay attention to the gauge and check it often throughout the project.

Anything can affect your gauge from how tired you are to having a spooky movie on. Checking your gauge often will help you avoid disappointment in the long run.

Fastening Off

When you've come to the end of your pattern and made your very last stitch, you'll need to cut your skein of yarn from the crocheted fabric and secure it. Why? If you don't fasten the yarn properly, to put it bluntly, your project...will...fall...apart. Maybe not today, maybe not tomorrow, maybe not even next Thursday, but it will happen sometime. I'm not psychic or I would have won the lottery by now.

Cut the yarn about 6 inches (15 cm) from the hook, yarn over, and pull the yarn all the way through the loop on your hook. Now pull the tail of the yarn gently to tighten the loop. This will prevent the accidental unraveling of your stitches, but it's still not enough. Do not overlook the next step or you'll look like a dog attacked you.

Weaving in the End(s)

Thread a large-eyed tapestry needle with the tail of your yarn. Working on the back of the fabric (so it won't show), weave the yarn through three or four stitches to lock it into place. Then weave back through the same stitches. If you are, like me, a worrier (or as my friend Laurie says, "a perfection enthusiast"), go up or down a row and repeat the weaving. Cut the yarn close to—but not up against—the crocheted fabric. Gently pull the fabric, and the yarn end will disappear into the stitches forever.

Acknowledgments

I'm amazed how many talented people had to pull together in this creative endeavor. I'd like to thank everyone at Lark Books for producing an amazing book! Special thanks go to my editor Terry Taylor, whose continuous enthusiasm for creating this book is apparent on every page—dude, you rock! Thanks too to Mark Bloom and Larry Shea for their editorial expertise. I owe another thank-you to Karen Manthey for doing a great job of technical editing; you polished the designs perfectly and made the process fun!

To Kate Epstein, my wonderful agent, thank you so much for your patience. I promise to call more often! Also, I could not have put together all these designs without the generosity of the yarn companies who provided their newest and best fibers for all the projects. Thank you! And an extra special thanks to the wonderful people who stitched and tested the designs (see Sample Test Crochetiers).

I cannot express enough gratitude to my best friend Gary, who supported this book when it was just an idea and gave me the encouragement and confidence I needed to follow it through. Finally, I want to dedicate this book and my career to the memory of my wonderful mom Dolores, whose incredible love and enduring life lessons live on in my designs.

A special thanks to the following businesses for their help with this book. All are located in Asheville, North Carolina, except where noted.

Photo Prop Loans

Hunk Men's Clothing and Accessories

Old North State Clothing Company

Dick's Sporting Goods

Photo Locations

Low Rider

Walnut Hill Tree Farm (Tuckasegee, NC)

Digable Pizza

Clothing Care Center

Tower Associates, Inc.

Southern Waterways

Flying Frog Café/The Frog Bar

Santé Wine Bar

Asheville Tourists Baseball

Joe King's Barber Shop

Sample Test Crochetiers

Gabriel Arregui: Pure Comfort
James Ashworth: Hurry Sundown
Bobby G. Atkinson, Jr.: Comforolled
Janette Atwell: Stock Sweater
Sherri Bondy: For the Prepsters
Peter Franzi: Metrocabled
Lisa Harris: Power Tie
Connie Hoffman: Dawg
Peggy Marcus: Saugatuck Winter
Joyce Nordstrom: Finale Argyle
Dick Worrall: Convertible Cover

Hooks for the Book

Hooks provided by G3 Studios (www.g3studios.net)

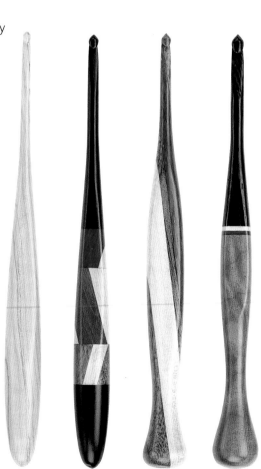

About the Author

Drew Emborsky's quirky title as "The Crochet Dude"—and his kitschy tongue-in-cheek designs—have propelled him from an unknown fiber artist to the cutting edge of the fiber design world. His role as a prominent male knitter and crochetier has opened doors for other men who were stuck in the closet with their yarn, knitting needles, and crochet hooks.

Drew has been featured in national magazines like *BUST, Crochet!, Interweave Crochet*, and *Knit.1*, as well as in international newspapers like London's *The Sunday Telegraph*. He has also appeared on numerous television programs, including *Knitty Gritty, Needlearts Studio, Uncommon Threads*, and *Paint Paper & Craft*. He is chairman of the Professional Development Committee of the Crochet Guild of America, which awarded him a master certificate in crochet. He studied fine arts at Kendall College of Art & Design in Grand Rapids, Michigan, and now lives in Houston, Texas, with his cats Chandler and Cleocatra.

Since launching his website (www.drewemborsky.com) in February 2005, Drew has gained a loyal international following. His blog (www.blog.thecrochetdude.com) receives thousands of visitors every day. You can find his patterns at www.lulu.com/thecrochetdude and peruse his merchandise at www.cafepress.com/thecrochetdude. Sign up for his newsletter at https://app.quicksizzle.com/survey.aspx?sfid=24923.

A Note on Suppliers

Usually, you can find the supplies you need for making the projects in Lark books at your local craft supply store, discount mart, home improvement center, or retail shop relevant to the topic of the book. Occasionally, however, you may need to buy materials or tools from specialty suppliers. In order to provide you with the most up-to-date information, we have created a listing of suppliers on our website, which we update on a regular basis. Visit us at www.larkbooks.com, click on "Sources," and then search for the relevant materials. You can also search by book title, vendor, and author name. Additionally, you can search for supply sources located in or near your town by entering your zip code. You will find numerous companies listed, with the web address and/or mailing address and phone number.

Index